American and Catholic

Clyde F. Crews

American and Catholic:

A Popular History of Catholicism
in the United States

ST. ANTHONY MESSENGER PRESS

Cincinnati, Ohio

Nihil Obstat: Rev. Lawrence Landini, O.F.M.
　　　　　　　Rev. Edward J. Gratsch

Imprimi Potest: Rev. John Bok, O.F.M.
　　　　　　　Provincial

Imprimatur: +Most Rev. Carl K. Moeddel
　　　　　　　Auxiliary Bishop and Vicar General
　　　　　　　Archdiocese of Cincinnati
　　　　　　　October 27, 1993

Cover and book design by Julie Lonneman

ISBN 0-86716-175-2

Foreword

This text emerges from a course on American religious thought I have been teaching at Bellarmine College in Louisville for nearly twenty years. I have also lectured on American religion to several parishes, Catholic and Episcopal, as part of their adult education programs.

I am grateful to the college for granting me release-time in 1991 to produce this book. To my students at the college and in the parishes, who have helped me to sharpen my thought by their insightful questions and suggestions, I am also grateful. My thanks go in a special way as well to Father James Hennesey, S.J., my mentor at Fordham University, whose teaching and writing in American Catholic studies have influenced me considerably.

I am particularly grateful to the editors and contributors of the *Catholic Historical Review* and the *U.S. Catholic Historian*. In preparing this volume, I have gone back and restudied their quarterly issues in order to take the pulse of recent scholarship in the American Catholic community.

Although I have worked with primary sources in my own preparation over the years, I am also deeply indebted to several particularly fine secondary source studies on which I have depended greatly for factual information and insight. They are listed in the Bibliography.

Contents

An Ancient Faith in a Modern Republic

In the World's Columbian Exposition, America rendered honor to herself among the nations. It now remains for those who kneel at the same altar before which Columbus knelt to complete his work by making of this republic a bright jewel in the crown of the Church.

These heady words come to us from a century-old book grandly titled *Lives of the Catholic Heroes and Heroines of America.* Written in conjunction with the World's Columbian Exposition, held in Chicago in 1893 to celebrate (a year late) Columbus' first landing in the New World four hundred years earlier, they bespeak a confident, almost cocky, attitude about the future of Catholicism in America.

With the 1992 quincentenary of the Columbus landing, we have learned as a people to be more restrained in our celebrations. Historical opinion, as the commemoration neared, gravitated wildly between seeing Columbus as a kind of savior for beginning the process that resulted in the American republic and, at the opposite pole, as a kind of Satan for exploiting the native people and for plundering the resources of the earth. Even when moderate historians seek a reading of the great discoverer somewhere on middle ground, it is clear that the nation cannot applaud the magical year of 1492 with the unrestrained glee of a century ago.

And yet, even in our more probing and questioning age, the five hundredth anniversary of Columbus' arrival on the Atlantic shores gives occasion for chastened rejoicing and critical analysis of life in this land over the centuries. Specifically, the time is ripe for reviewing Catholicism in the

Christopher Columbus, depicted in a Venetian mosaic.

1

United States—the most powerful nation yet to arise within the geographical arc of Columbus' discovery; to explore the influence of the faith that, at least in part, motivated the famous Italian on his voyage and to examine the influence the national life has had upon that faith.

Catholicism was present at the creation of the American colonial enterprise: in the Spanish settlements of the South and the West; in the pious French missionaries in what is now the Midwest; in the stalwart English colonists who came to Maryland, extending toleration to other faiths in the process. As the eastern colonies moved toward nationhood in the late eighteenth century, the faith was substantially represented in the patriot ranks, even though Catholics themselves made up only a small percentage of the population. Within two generations, due largely to an enormous inflow of immigrants, Catholics would constitute the largest single religious denomination in the country.

The story of Catholics in the American nation is, then, impressive. Because the United States was the first nation to invent itself, to separate Church and State, to consider itself a missionary of liberty to the nations, it is vital to chronicle the impact of Catholicism on the life of the country.

A vast quantity of historical literature exists in this field, most recently produced by such scholars as Jay Dolan, John Tracy Ellis and James Hennesey. (A more complete listing can be found in the Bibliography.) This brief account will attempt to present many of the major personalities, movements, spiritualities, conflicts, changes and constancies within the American Catholic community. Additionally, it will seek to examine the impact that the United States and Catholicism have had upon one another.

Through the centuries, Catholicism has learned important American lessons and values: liberty, participation, toleration, due process and pluralism. Similarly, the United States seems to have benefited from the Catholic presence, with its long insistence on rootedness, ritual, tradition, balance, organization, institutionalized earnestness, the sacramental and incarnational, and respect for evidence and intellect. State and Church have, in short, enriched one another. Each has, at times, found itself trapped by narrowness and a falling away from its high ideals. Thus have they learned, side by side, something of humility and the need for ongoing reform.

Catholicism has been described by its defenders as a "sleeping giant" in American life, with enormous powers for the good waiting to be more fully unleashed. Especially in the wake of the Second Vatican Council, we no longer speak rhetorically of America as a bright jewel in the Church's crown. And yet a faithful and self-critical Catholicism possesses a treasure that it still may share with America and Americans.

American Catholicism is still in some ways a sleeping giant: large, gangly, diverse, occasionally perplexed and perplexing. But it is laden with possibilities, latent with values and instincts that could help to revivify a people. I hope that this book will show this ancient faith in its rich complexity as it lives within and influences the American nation.

Part One

Before the Revolution: Far-Flung Catholicism

Chapter One

The Land and the Native Americans

The United States today is a patchwork quilt of religious beliefs and practices. Its landscape is punctuated with a dizzying variety of temples, mosques and churches of many traditions. This should hardly be surprising in the nation that pioneered toleration and the separation of Church and State in the modern era.

Even Catholicism, the largest single denomination in the nation, shows a wide range of architectural diversity: the Gothic splendor of St. Patrick's Cathedral in New York; the striking modernity of San Francisco's St. Mary's Cathedral; the mission churches of California and the Southwest; the stark Cistercian simplicity of the abbey church of the Kentucky Trappists; the onion-dome ethnic spires of the industrial Northeast; the storefront chapels of Appalachia.

Tahoma, "the Mountain that was God" (Mt. Ranier in Washington's Cascades).

Before any of the European faiths appeared on the scene from the early sixteenth century onward, the North American continent already revealed a geography of holiness. The Native American people had called this continent home for thousands of years before European explorers arrived. Traditional wisdom has long held that the people later known as Indians began to cross into North America some fifteen to twenty thousand years ago on a land bridge now under the Bering Strait, which links Siberia to Alaska. More recent archaeological finds in Pennsylvania and New Mexico nearly double the length of time that human life has been on this continent and may cause a revision in the theory.

Historians can only guess at numbers, but most estimate that some fifteen to twenty million people were living in the New World when Columbus arrived. No more than one to two million would have dwelt in what is now the United States.

7

Their influence lingers in our lives. These Native Americans presented a smorgasbord of new foods to the world: corn, potatoes, tomatoes, pumpkins, peanuts, squash and many strains of beans. Over half of the fifty states in the Union today bear names that have their roots in Indian names and words.

For Discussion

Trace Native American influence where you live. What tribes inhabited your area, and where are they now? What sites, place names, local crops, etc., stand as reminders of their presence?

To summarize what these peoples were like is a difficult enterprise. They were diverse in language and culture. Some civilizations, such as the Mayan and Aztec to the south of the United States, were highly advanced technically, although at times given to particularly hideous human sacrifice. Some groups fought only in self-defense; others were more aggressive. Some lived amid plenty with highly developed arts; others lived in poverty, eking out a meager living from season to season. Many American Indian habits depicted by Hollywood—war paint, scalping, the cult of the medicine man—are not unique to Native Americans but can be found in many cultures outside the western hemisphere.

Although the Native Americans also were diverse in religious belief and practice, some common traits appear. They accepted an unseen world of gods, demons, spirits and powers that undergirded and sustained the world that is seen and sensed. A mighty force stood within and beyond them. To the Sioux it was *wakan*; to the Iroquois, *orenda*; to the Algonquins, *manitou*. Like people in practically all cultures, they found such spirit or power both attractive and terrifying. They got in touch with such power, and it with them, through nature, dreams, animals, the tribe and specially gifted individuals.

Countless rituals enabled the individual to become part of that wider and lasting reality, to draw nurture and strength from it. Belief in a continuation of this life into another world or realm was quite common. Among the Iroquois there was a priesthood of three men and three women who were called "keepers of the faith." The "vision quest" of many tribes is but one method by which young initiates sought out spiritual experiences and visions through fasting, mortification and trances.

One factor that became—and remains—quite dominant in Native American spirituality is a profound sense of place. The earth itself became something very like a sacrament to these people. Throughout the United States today one may still visit regions that have been specially venerated among the Indians of North America: the Navajo Place of Emergence in the Four

Native American Faiths

When the European Christians arrived in America, they came face-to-face with a Native American people whose systems of belief had been deep-set for centuries. As one reads the accounts of Pueblo and Navajo religion by the historian of the Native Americans, Alvin M. Josephy, Jr., in The Indian Heritage in America, *one can imagine the feelings of the first Christian missionaries at encountering such beliefs—feelings of strangeness, and yet perhaps a certain familiarity with the color, pageantry and significance of it all.*

The Pueblo People

The Pueblo communities were closely knit units in which, for the sake of solidarity and the welfare of all, the individual was subordinated to the group; ...individualistic qualities, competitiveness, aggressiveness and the ambition to lead were looked on as offensive to the supernatural powers....

Religion was a daily experience, permeating all of life, and acting as a principal integrating force among the people. Associated with all acts, it was rich in myth and symbol and was dramatized by a year-round succession of elaborate ceremonials that utilized imaginative and beautiful costumes and included songs, poetry and rites....

Observing religion occupied much of the people's time; Pueblo men, indeed, are said to have devoted at least half their time to religious activities.... There were numerous deities as well as benevolent spirits, called kachinas, who visited the Pueblo people for six months each year as messengers of the gods.

The Navajo People

At the heart of Navajo existence is the desire to keep one's life in harmony with the supernatural and with the universe. The Navajos acquired many ritual elements from the Pueblos, but fitted them to their own...religious ideas. The universe, according to the Navajos, contains mortals, called the Earth Surface People, and supernatural beings, the Holy People, who possess power that can help or harm a mortal. The latter, it is believed, can bring about or restore harmony in the universe...by the performance of ceremonies and rituals, meticulously preserved and carried out.

A Mohawk Prayer

O Great Spirit, creator of all things:
Human beings, trees, grass, berries,
Help us, be kind to us.
Let us be happy on earth.
Let us lead our children
To a good life and old age.
These our people:
   give them good minds
To love one another.
O Great Spirit,
Be kind to us.
Give these people the favor
To see green trees,
Green grass, flowers and berries
This next spring;
So we all meet again,
O great Spirit,
We ask of you.

—Anonymous (from *American Indian Prayers and Poetry*, edited by J. Ed Sharpe)

Corners section of the Southwest; Tahoma, the "Mountain that was God," some 14,000 feet above Puget Sound in the Pacific Northwest; a rock foundation sacred to the Seneca on Canandaigua Lake in New York state's Finger Lakes.

In addition to such natural sites, Native Americans in the centuries before Columbus also constructed large and intricate formations of cosmic significance. Concentric earthen ridges built some three thousand years ago at Poverty Point, Louisiana, are called by some a New World Stonehenge. Cahokia Mounds near St. Louis are massive earth-rises that served the religious needs of over ten thousand people in the thirteenth century. Serpent-shaped mounds twist across the Ohio landscape.

Human settlement in the Southwest dates back well before the time of Christ. By the sixteenth century, the region evidenced a settled way of life that depended on agriculture as well as on hunting and gathering. The Native Americans the first Spanish encountered in the American Southwest were a diverse group with keen political and community-building skills, as the Pueblo culture in particular demonstrates. In *The Indian Heritage of America*, historian Alvin Josephy, Jr., reports that some sixteen thousand people were living in about eighty compact settlements when the Spanish first arrived. The buildings, constructed of stone or adobe, often overlooked a central plaza. (The Zuni in western New Mexico still live in such a community.)

These people of developed spiritualities drew a large influx of European Catholic missionaries to the New World from the late fifteenth century onward. Although never massively successful in terms of numbers, those early priests nonetheless managed to convert thousands to the Christian faith. Unfortunately, the Good News was delivered in an evangelistic style that at times rode roughshod over native cultures and rites. Some of the missions were repressive as well as liberating.

It is important to avoid stereotyping either side in the early encounter between Native Americans and the Spanish. Some missionaries were sensitive to native languages and culture patterns; many were not. Many native cultures were peaceful; others were not. The Spanish did try to impose their cultural heritage, complete with residential, behavioral and faith patterns. The mission church was the geographic center of the communities they established, as well as a center of authority and organization; it offered education, health care and an introduction to European culture.

When Pope John Paul II visited Phoenix, Arizona, in September 1987, he conducted a special meeting with Native Americans. As reported in *Origins*, the pope remarked to his hearers that history would record "the deeply positive aspects" of their early meeting with European culture. And yet, the pontiff added, "that encounter was a harsh and painful reality. The cultural oppression, the injustices, the disruption of your life and of your traditional societies must be acknowledged." Speaking on behalf of the Indian community on that same occasion, Alfretta M. Antone, vice president of the Pima-Maricopa Indian Community, asked Pope John Paul to support her people so that "our sacred ways...be respected."

Detail of a mural by Diego Rivera, showing Spanish exploitation of native peoples.

A Pope Addresses Native Americans in Phoenix, Arizona (1987)

The first Native American candidate proposed for canonization, Kateri Tekakwitha, was born near Auriesville, New York, about 1656. Her mother was an Algonquin who had accepted Christianity and her father a chief of the Mohawks. A smallpox epidemic orphaned the young girl, left her disfigured and impaired her vision. Taken into an uncle's home, she there first encountered Catholic missionaries. At the age of ten, she was baptized with the name Kateri on Easter Sunday, 1676. Her short life of austerity and service ended in 1680.

The best-known witness of Christian holiness among the native people of North America is Kateri Tekakwitha, whom I had the privilege, seven years ago, of declaring "blessed" and of holding her up to the whole church and the world as an outstanding example of Christian life. Even when she dedicated herself fully to Christ, to the point of taking the prophetic step of making a vow of perpetual virginity, she always remained what she was, a true daughter of her people, following her tribe in hunting seasons and continuing her devotions in the environment most suited to her way of life, before a rough cross carved by herself in the forest.—Pope John Paul II

For Discussion

Discuss the relationship between ecological concerns and Native American spirituality.

Over the last generation, American Catholicism has sought to respect more fully the Native American ways. Many people have been laboring to bring greater justice and sensitivity to relationships with Native Americans on behalf of both Church and society. In 1991 one religious community much involved in Canadian Indian evangelization, the Missionary Oblates of Mary Immaculate, offered a corporate apology to native people for often overriding native language, tradition and religion.

The official 1990 census calculated the number of Native Americans at 1.9 million. Of these, Church sources report some 285,000 Catholic Indians in the United States. The dioceses with the largest numbers of Native Americans include Santa

Statue of Kateri Tekakwitha presented by the Bureau of Catholic Indian Missions to the Shrine of the Immaculate Conception, Washington, D.C., in 1992.

Fe, New Mexico; Gallup, New Mexico; Tucson, Arizona; Santa Rosa, California; Rapid City, South Dakota; and Great Falls-Billings, Montana. One of the most visible spokespersons for Native American Catholics today is Bishop Donald Pelotte of Gallup, himself a Native American.

In a 1977 statement, *The Church and American Indians: Towards Dialogue and Respect*, the bishops of the United States revealed a heightened understanding of Native American values, needs and aspirations. Some dioceses have recently established special offices for ministry to Native Americans, while financial assistance has been tendered through the Campaign for Human Development and such agencies as the Commission for Catholic Missions among the Colored People and the Indians (founded in 1885) and the Bureau of Catholic Indian Missions (dating from 1907).

Religious communities continue their work in many missions, especially in the Southwest. Several mission schools have been transferred to tribal operation and dialogues have been initiated between missionaries and Native American leaders. In recent years such groups as the Federation of Catholic Indian Leaders and the Native American Native Religious (NANR) have come to birth.

Over the last generation, the Catholic people in the United States have become increasingly conscious of serious poverty and complex social problems among American Indians; they have also learned of the accomplishment, poise and initiative of many leaders in the Indian community. And they have come to realize that the men and women of the Native American communities of this country are far more than just victims who receive help. Rather, they are parties to a dialogue in which both sides find enrichment. Some of this enrichment is evidenced in a more intense interest in Native American spirituality. The once seemingly arcane world of chant, dance, spirits and vision quests of the Indian people is vividly examined in scores of titles that once would not have passed an editor's desk.

Indians stand forward in the nation today as proud Americans in their own right. For people of all faiths, they also serve as reminders of the ongoing need for national self-scrutiny in the ways of justice, and of the personal search for harmony and holiness in the ways of the earth and the heart.

Chapter Two

Spanish Friars in the New World

For nearly two hundred fifty years before the 1776 signing of the Declaration of Independence, North America was explored, conquered and settled by European powers. Coming with these colonizers, Catholicism made its influence felt in three geographical areas, each ruled by a different power: a Spanish band reaching along the Gulf Coast from Florida into the Southwest and up into California; the French central strip along the Mississippi River and around the Great Lakes; the British colonies along the Atlantic seaboard.

In his four voyages to the New World on behalf of Spain, Columbus never set foot on the North American mainland. That task awaited later Spanish explorers such as Ponce de Leon, who first landed in Florida in 1513. And yet the island of Puerto Rico, which Columbus discovered on his second voyage in 1493, boasts the oldest Catholic diocese that is now part of the United States. Julius II, pope at the time Luther posted his famous Ninety-Five Theses in 1517, established the Diocese of Puerto Rico (later renamed the Diocese of San Juan) in 1511. Alonso Manso of Salamanca, Spain, headed the new see, thus becoming the first resident Catholic bishop in the New World.

Throughout the sixteenth century, Spain had become the dominant power on the European scene. Under the leadership of the Hapsburgs Charles V (1516-1556) and Phillip II (1556-1598), Catholic Spain experienced a golden age of art, literature and spirituality. In this century there emerged, in the wake of the reforms of Cardinal Francisco Ximenez de Cisneros (1436-1517), a trio of mystics, saints and reformers: Teresa of Avila (1515-1582), John of the Cross (1552-1591) and Ignatius Loyola (1491-1556). Out of this era of Spanish energy, intensity—and, sometimes, moral insensitivity—the

A mural at the Indian burial grounds at Fountain of Youth Archaeological Park in St. Augustine shows Spanish Franciscans burying converts.

earliest European settlements in the New World took form.

Throughout the sixteenth century, the explorers and conquerors of Spain concentrated on taking control of the New World from the native peoples. By the late 1530's the Spanish flag flew over most of Mexico, Central and South America—all except Brazil, which was taken by the Portuguese. And for most of the colonial period (up into the nineteenth century) the Spanish lands in the modern-day United States were little more than outposts of Mexico.

The motivation of the Spanish of this epoch was undoubtedly mixed, mingling a wish for wealth, land and empire with an earnest desire on the part of many to spread the Catholic faith to two continents of natives who had never heard of the gospel. Especially in the light of the Reformation, many were to see the New World as a prime locale for the triumph of Catholicism. According to Catholic historian Jay P. Dolan in *The American Catholic Experience*, the faith of both the Spanish conquistador and friar was "an intensely fervent and fanatically vigorous religion.... Sixteenth-century Spain was becoming an increasingly closed society, intolerant of racial or religious diversity."

While the Spanish initially turned their attention on the richer and more developed lands south of the present United States, later in the sixteenth century they cast their eyes as well toward the "borderlands" that make up part of that country today. For this reason, the earliest history of Catholicism in America takes on a Spanish flavor.

Highly dedicated missionaries from the Iberian peninsula labored along the southern Atlantic shore and the Gulf Coast and into the Southwest and California. In the sixteenth century these early priests had visited and sometimes attempted missions (without great success) in lands that were to become such states as South Carolina, Florida, Georgia and Mississippi.

Florida originally saw the greatest missionary activity. As part of his mandate to his explorers, King Charles V had ordered that Indians be taught "our holy Catholic Faith." Accordingly, priests came along on Ponce de Leon's second voyage to Florida in 1521. Though they met with little success, the records of their religious labors form the earliest authentic record of priestly activity on the North American mainland.

A Dominican priest, Luis Cancer, tried to evangelize

For Discussion

Discuss the impact, positive and negative, of the Spanish missions on a hunting and gathering society.

A reconstruction of Mission Nombre de Dios stands where the Spanish landed and founded St. Augustine in 1565.

Florida's Indians in 1549, only to meet with martyrdom for his efforts. The Church took more substantial root with the establishment of St. Augustine in 1565. On August 28 of that year, an expedition led by Pedro Menendez first sighted land and named the new settlement for the saint honored on that day, Augustine of Hippo. Its church, *Nombre de Dios* ("Name of God"), thus became the oldest parish in the continental United States.

In the late 1560's, Jesuit missionaries arrived in Florida and began the work of opening additional mission stations. Eight of these men were to die at the hands of their would-be converts, and the survivors were recalled in 1572. The very next year Spanish Franciscans came to the area to resume the work.

By the mid 1650's, some thirty Franciscan missions were in place. In 1674 St. Augustine witnessed a grand liturgical spectacle: Seven men were ordained to the priesthood. Until the time that Florida was turned over to the English in 1763, some three hundred Franciscan friars were involved in spreading the gospel; their converts have been estimated to number some thirty thousand Indians. Under English rule, however, the mission areas came under attack, and Catholic activity in Florida became but a shadow of what it had been under the Spanish.

Farther west, in modern-day Texas, Arizona and New Mexico, Spanish colonization and missionary activity was sparse until the early seventeenth century. One notable exception was the mission of Franciscan Juan de Padilla (1500-1542). He traveled with Francisco Coronado's expedition into what is now New Mexico, and decided to stay behind to spread the faith to the native peoples when the rest of the party returned south. Padilla was well received by the Quivira Indians, but soon met up with a hostile tribe who put him to death in Kansas in 1542. In American Catholic history, he has come to be known as the proto-martyr, the first to give his life for the faith in territory that is now the United States.

Ongoing Spanish Catholic presence in the American Southwest began in 1598. In the new century, mission activity intensified in New Mexico, especially with the foundation of the town of Santa Fe in 1610. The settlement took its name ("Holy Faith") from the military camp near Grenada where Ferdinand and Isabella had defeated the Moors in Spain. At Santa Fe today, one may visit the hallowed San Miguel Chapel.

The New Mexico Missions in 1634

In the following passage, dated February 12, 1634, Franciscan Father Alonso de Benevides reports on the missions of New Mexico. (In this same year, 1634, the Ark *and the* Dove *arrived in Maryland, establishing the first significant English Catholic settlement in America.)*

More than twenty Indians, devoted to the service of the Church, live with [the priest]. They take turns in relieving one another as porters, sextons, cooks, bell-ringers, gardeners, refectioners, and in other roles. They perform their duties with as much circumspection and care as if they were friars. At eventide they say their prayers together with much devotion in front of some image.

In every pueblo where a friar resides, he has schools for the teaching of praying, singing, playing musical instruments, and other interesting things. Promptly at dawn one of the Indian singers...goes to ring the bell for Prime, at the sound of which those who go to school assemble and sweep the rooms thoroughly. The singers chant Prime in the choir. The friar must be present at all of this, and takes notes of those who have failed to perform this duty to reprimand them later.... Mass over..., all kneel down by the church door and sing the *Salve* in their own tongue.

At mealtime, the poor people in the pueblo who are not ill come to the porter's lodge, where the cooks...have sufficient food ready, which is served to them by the friar; food for the sick is sent to their homes. After mealtime, it always happens that the friar has to go to some neighboring pueblo to hear a confession or to see if they are careless in the boys' school.

In the evening, they toll the bell for Vespers, which are chanted by the singers who are on duty for the week, and according to the importance of the feast they celebrate it with organ chants as they do for Mass. (from *Documents of American Catholic History*, edited by John Tracy Ellis)

Mission San Miguel, built about 1610, is generally regarded as the oldest chapel in the United States.

With a construction date of approximately 1610, the core structure is the oldest chapel in the United States.

The Franciscans seemed quite successful in their establishments, including stations in the mesa towns of the Hopi. By the 1630's, over one hundred fifty churches served the scattered pueblos of the region. The number of converts soared into the thousands. Then, in an uprising known as the Pueblo Revolt of 1680, Native Americans who had generally been known as peaceful people rebelled against the Spanish. The deaths of over four hundred Spanish settlers as well as more than twenty Franciscans resulted. Aided by Jesuits, the Franciscan priests were later able to recover much of their work, with the exception of the Hopi region. A report by a Franciscan visitor to New Mexico in 1776 noted the existence of twenty-four missions, twenty clergy and over eighteen thousand Spanish and Indian believers.

Beginning around 1750, folk artists among New Mexico Catholics began to craft the *santos*, carved wood statues that portrayed Jesus, Mary and the saints. Originally intended for churches or private devotion, these figures, so striking in their simplicity and directness, are not only prized possessions of museums in the American West, but also a testament to the deep belief and devotion of ordinary believers of the colonial era. To this day, Hispanic Catholicism in the United States is

Fra Junipero Serra, who established a string of nine missions along the coast of California from San Diego to San Francisco.

For Discussion

Some Native Americans protested the September 1988 beatification of Fra Junipero Serra, charging him with mistreating Indians. Research the arguments and discuss how culture and times affect concepts of holiness.

suffused with tenderness and deep veneration for the Madonna and the saints.

The most famous pioneer priest in early Arizona was Eusebio Francisco Kino (1645-1711), a Jesuit born in the Italian Tyrol. A scholar in the fields of mathematics and astronomy, Kino provided critically needed mapping skills in the areas where he served. Kino baptized thousands, taught agricultural skills to his people and moved quickly across Arizona, establishing a succession of missions, most notably San Francisco Xavier del Bec. His statue stands in Statuary Hall in the Capitol in Washington, placed there by the State of Arizona. Jesuit and Franciscan priests continued to serve throughout the early part of the Spanish colonial era, although the mid-eighteenth century was a time of decline rather than growth. In fact, from the 1780's through the 1860's, Arizona was practically devoid of Catholic clergy.

Despite unavailing attempts by priests in the late seventeenth century, Texas was not to have permanent Catholic settlements until the early eighteenth century, most notably the mission of San Antonio, established in 1718. The best known of the early Texas missionaries was Franciscan Antonio Margil (1657-1726), a man renowned as an educator who established colleges for the training of missionaries. Noted for his sanctity and power of preaching, Margil was declared Venerable by Pope Gregory XVI in 1836.

In the popular imagination of most Americans, to speak of Spanish Catholicism in America is to conjure up images of the California missions, complete with adobe structures and brown-robed friars. In the last generation, however, the system of missions has come under increasing historical scrutiny as historians raise questions of Spanish sensitivity to native cultures and peoples. A structure of community living once uncritically saluted is now being probed for signs of domination and even repression.

European settlement and Catholicism came relatively late to California. It began on July 16, 1769, with the establishment of a mission at San Diego, one of nine founded by Franciscan Junipero Serra (1713-1784). This best-known of all the California missionaries had entered the Franciscan order at age seventeen, coming to the missions of Mexico while in his late thirties. Noted for his piety and the apostolic simplicity of his life-style, Serra took up residence at the San Carlos Mission in

Junipero Serra Reports From Monterey, California

Hail Jesus, Mary, Joseph! On the most solemn feast of the Holy Spirit, Pentecost Sunday, June 3, 1770, this mission of San Carlos de Monterey was founded to the joy of the sea and land expeditions. In a short time the rejoicing was shared by the entire kingdom and eagerly celebrated in both Spains.

On that day, after imploring the assistance of the Holy Spirit, the sacred standard of the cross was blessed, raised, and adored by all. The ground was blessed, an altar set up, and a sort of chapel formed with naval flags. The holy sacrifice of the Mass was sung, a sermon was preached, and, at the end, the *Te Deum* was intoned. With these [ceremonies], possession was duly taken of Monterey for holy Church and the Crown of Spain.... (from *Documents of American Catholic History*, edited by John Tracy Ellis)

Carmel, where he lies buried today. Like the Jesuit Kino of Arizona, the Franciscan Serra is commemorated in the Hall of Statuary in the Capitol at Washington.

In all, between 1769 and 1821, twenty-one missions were built in a chain spreading north up the California coast. They stood like pearls on a string along the famous *El Camino Real*, the "Royal Road" celebrated by Pope John Paul II in his visit to California's Carmel Mission in 1987. Until the 1840's, these establishments represented practically the only Christian centers in all of California. Some one hundred and fifty Franciscan priests were involved in the work, and nearly one hundred thousand baptisms were recorded.

Each mission itself, of course, was considerably more than a church reserved for worship alone. Rather, the mission was a complex which, in addition to offering sacraments and spirituality, served educational, agricultural, social and medical needs. At Santa Barbara, some two hundred fifty family dwellings were attached to the mission. Over fifty trades were taught. Festivals were celebrated with gusto. At most of the missions, protection was provided from the attacks of hostile Indians.

But there was a dark side, too. Runaways were likely to be sought out and brought back to the compound. The lash and stocks were used to punish those who broke community rules.

Originally, the concept of the mission was that it would serve as a kind of protection and training center to "civilize" the native people. Within ten years, so the idealist theory went at the time, this work could be accomplished, and the residents could move to a more regular structure of life as part of the traditional Catholic parish. Rarely do ideals and realities meet. And they did not do so in the missions of California.

Was the mission system in California—or, indeed, throughout the Spanish empire in America—repressive? In candor, most historians today, using the measure of contemporary sensibility, would answer with a qualified yes. Was good also accomplished within their precincts? Again, from most historians, there would be a qualified affirmative. No less a figure than Pope John Paul II, as we have seen, readily admitted that injustices were clearly inflicted on the Native Americans in their encounter with colonial Christianity.

According to historian Jay Dolan, the missions of California were to be distinguished from their contemporaries

The Mission of Santa Barbara, California, founded in 1786, housed several hundred Indians, who farmed under the direction of the friars.

in Texas, New Mexico or Arizona largely because of the striking economic success that accompanied their religious fervor. The average California mission involved at least five hundred Indians, who, under the direction of the friars, raised cattle and planted orchards and vineyards. By the 1830's, the agricultural value of the system was placed at over seventy-five million dollars. Over fifty thousand Indians were converted at these California centers over a span of two generations.

Yet historians reckon that diseases (many of them new maladies brought by white settlers), hard work and soaring infant mortality rates decimated the Native American population. By the 1830's, the Indian population of the area was only one-fourth what it had been sixty years before. When Mexico became an independent nation in 1821, it soon spread its control to California, dissolving the missions and appropriating their land.

When John Carroll became bishop of Baltimore in 1789, he estimated the number of Catholics under his jurisdiction in the eastern part of the United States to be twenty-five thousand. The number of Catholics at the same time in California and the Southwest was approximately the same.

This western region would not enter the United States until the 1840's. And yet it is important to recall that Hispanic Catholicism in the West, at the nation's beginning, was a significant force with a substantial tradition behind it. As we will see in Chapter Twelve, the number of Hispanic Catholics in America would again become proportionately large in the twentieth century.

In addition to planting the ancient faith in the western portion of New World America, the Spanish settlers and missionaries left their mark on American geography and place names. Busy American executives flying into San Francisco, San Diego, San Antonio or Los Angeles might recall that they enter cities first established by the Spanish in honor of Francis, James, Anthony and the angels. Visitors to the Atlantic beaches near St. Augustine frolic in an area that Spaniards dedicated to the memory of the North African saint. Campers in the Sangre de Cristo mountain range from Colorado to New Mexico take their leisure in lands that Hispanics named in honor of the Blood of Christ.

But the Catholic Church in America was not homogeneous. Rather, even a brief study of colonial Catholicism from the sixteenth through eighteenth centuries reveals a diverse weave of English, French and Spanish traditions, enriched by the labor, piety and steadfastness of thousands of Native Americans. Even before the American nation was formed in the Revolutionary era, the ancient faith in the area now known as the United States constituted something of a Catholic League of Nations.

For Discussion

Divide your group into conquistadors, friars and Native Americans. Role-play an evaluation of one another's life-styles.

Chapter Three

Catholic France Weighs In

During the sixteenth century, mighty Spain had the exploration of the American lands largely to itself. With France's rise to European dominance in the seventeenth century came the turn of the French explorers and missionaries to probe the vast western continent. The Gallic adventurers turned to lands not yet eyed by the Spanish, however; rarely did the Spanish and French meet in colonial America.

The French Catholic priests who came to the New World in the seventeenth and eighteenth centuries, like the Spanish before them, emerged from a veritable cauldron of intense piety and a longing—as they perceived it—to civilize and serve native people. In France this was the age of Vincent de Paul (1580-1660), Francis de Sales (1567-1622), Jane Frances de Chantal (1571-1641) and Jean-Jacques Olier (1608-1657), whose Society of St. Sulpice would have a marked influence on later American Catholic clerical leadership.

Thus, like the Spanish mission to America, the French movement was born from heightened spiritual zeal and self-sacrifice. Had the American explorations taken place in an earlier era of weak enthusiasm such as the later Middle Ages (the fourteenth century) or later, in the more skeptical age of the eighteenth-century Enlightenment, the situation of religion in America might have been quite different.

The French headquartered their colonial outposts in Canada, especially in Quebec City after 1608 and Montreal after 1642. A flourishing Catholic colony and culture eventually came to life in the young towns; but the restless French were eager to continue their explorations of the mid-continent. Before the century had ended, the explorers, often accompanied by clergy, had spread in what is now the northern tier of American states: along the Great Lakes and St. Lawrence River from Minnesota to Maine. In such well-known

Eastern North America as it appears on Father Louis Hennepin's second map, 1697.

Explorer René de la Salle explored the Mississippi from St. Louis to New Orleans, establishing the French claim to the Louisiana Territory.

For Discussion

The Iroquois, who inflicted hideous torture on their enemies, are depicted in fiction and folklore as cruel and vindictive. At the same time, the League of Five Nations was a great experiment in peaceful cooperation; Benjamin Franklin proposed it as the model for the union of the colonies when the Constitution was being written. What in the history of your nation and your Church would you like to see treasured? What remembered with pain?

treks along the Mississippi as those of Jesuit Jacques Marquette or layman René de la Salle, they extended French influence along that waterway south to the Gulf of Mexico.

A Belgian Franciscan Recollet Father, Louis Hennepin (1626-1705), accompanied la Salle on some of his western explorations and aided in mapping much of the upper Mississippi. His later writings on America were immensely popular in Europe. Hennepin could at times be slashingly critical of Native Americans. His words reveal a mindset all too common among Europeans of his age: "It must be granted that it is necessary to spend many years and undergo a great deal of pains to civilize a People so extremely stupid and barbarous" (*Documents of American Catholic History*, edited by John Tracy Ellis).

In the 1640's, while Spanish missions already flourished in Florida and New Mexico, French Jesuit Isaac Jogues (1607-1646) undertook successful work among Hurons at Sault Sainte Marie, Michigan. On a trip to Quebec in 1642, he was captured by Iroquois, members of a five-tribe confederation known as the Five Nations, and put to extraordinary torture which left him with mutilated hands.

Rescued by the Dutch, Jogues was taken to their settlement at New Amsterdam (later New York City), where he could find but two Roman Catholics in the young settlement, and later returned to France. Within two years, the extraordinary Jesuit was back in Quebec, eager to set out on a new mission. In the autumn of 1646, near Auriesville, New York, he was seized by a band of Mohawks, one of the Five Nations. Three months shy of his fortieth birthday, he was tomahawked to death. A lay companion, Jean de la Lande, died in the same way. Another lay assistant, physician René Goupil, had met a remarkably similar fate near the same locale in September, 1642.

These three stalwart missioners are among the eight designated by the Catholic Church as the North American Martyrs and declared saints in 1930. All of them met their death from hostile Indians in the 1640's in either New York or Canada. Two of these Jesuits—Jean de Brébeuf and Gabriel Lalemant—endured what may be the most grisly recorded tortures and deaths of any martyrs in the long history of Catholicism. While they still lived, their hearts were taken from their chests, their blood drunk and their limbs roasted.

The missionary priests were not the only believers of this

Hennepin's sketch of La Salle's landing in Texas to establish a colony at the behest of Louis XIV. Within four years, La Salle was murdered by his own men.

epoch to yield up their lives in order to affirm their Christian faith. A Huron convert, Stephen Tegananokoa, endured torture and death at the hands of hostile Cayuga Indians. Similarly, Margaret Garangouas, daughter of a chief, was tortured and then burned to death in defense of her new-found Christian faith. Both have been proposed for canonization as saints of the Church.

In the middle decades of the seventeenth century, Capuchin priests were active in New Brunswick, Canada, and present-day Maine. Missionaries in New York saw greater success beginning in the late 1660's among the Mohawks and Eries. Some two thousand baptisms occurred, including that of Kateri

Jean de Brébeuf, S.J., Instructs Missionaries to the Indians—1637

You must have sincere affection for the Savages—looking upon them as ransomed by the blood of the Son of God, and as our brethren with whom we are to pass the rest of our lives.

To conciliate the savages, you must be careful never to make them wait for you in embarking.

You must provide yourself with a tinder box or with a burning mirror, or with both, to furnish them with fire in the daytime to light their pipes, and in the evening when they have to encamp; these little services win their hearts.

....You must bear with their imperfections without saying a word, yes, even without seeming to notice them. Even if it is necessary to criticize anything, it must be done modestly, and with words and signs that evince love and not aversion. In short, you must try to be, and to appear always, cheerful.

....Jesus Christ is our true greatness; it is He alone and His Cross that should be sought in running after these people, for if you strive for anything else, you will find naught but bodily and spiritual affliction. But having found Jesus Christ in His Cross, you have found the roses in the thorns, sweetness in bitterness, all in nothing. (from *Documents of American Catholic History*, edited by John Tracy Ellis)

Tekakwitha, beatified in 1980.

In Michigan, Jesuits labored along the Straits of Mackinac in the 1640's and 1650's. But it was especially due to the work of Jesuit Father Jacques Marquette (1637-1675), who established posts at Sault Sainte Marie on the Upper Peninsula in 1668 and at St. Ignace in 1671, that Catholicism took firm root in Michigan. Marquette (whose likeness has joined that of Kino and Serra in Washington's Statuary Hall) accompanied Louis Joliet's expedition to explore the Mississippi in 1673. Shortly thereafter, he founded a mission among the Illinois, only to die of disease in his late thirties in 1675. Hurons and other tribes around Fort Pontchartrain (Detroit) were served by Franciscans from the beginning of the eighteenth century.

Wisconsin was also a fertile ground for French clerics in this era. Jesuit René Menard offered the first Mass in Wisconsin in 1661. His confrere Father Claude Allouez established the mission of St. Francis Xavier at Green Bay in 1669. For the next half century, it was a center from which clerics traveled to preach to nearby Indian tribes.

The most intense new evangelization took place in the lower reaches of New France, along the Mississippi Basin, in the late seventeenth century. The first mission in the Mississippi Valley, Immaculate Conception, was established for Illinois Indians along the upper branches of the Illinois River by Marquette shortly before his death in 1675. Succeeding Marquette at Immaculate Conception was the resourceful Allouez, who is said to have baptized over ten thousand Indians.

Louis Joliet and Jesuit Father Jacques Marquette launch an expedition to explore the Mississippi in 1673.

For Discussion

Compare the approaches used by the Spanish friars, the French Jesuits and today's missionaries. What strengths and weaknesses mark each?

Priests from Quebec going to minister to the Tamaroa tribe established the parish of Holy Family at Cahokia in present-day Illinois in 1699. Kaskaskia (Illinois) followed as a mission center in 1703, with Vincennes, on the Wabash in Indiana, hosting a parish from 1749. In Missouri, St. Louis was founded in 1764, with Jesuit missioner Sebastian Meurin as its first pastor.

French Catholic activity reached the Gulf Coast around the turn of the century. The Biloxi, Mississippi, area saw its first priest in 1699 and Mobile, Alabama, witnessed the beginning of a parish in 1703. With the founding of New Orleans in 1718 and the consequent beginning of St. Louis parish, Catholicism found a major center. The first sisters in America, the Ursulines from Rouen, France, came to New Orleans to found a girls' academy in 1727.

In 1763 the Treaty of Paris ended the French and Indian Wars, a series of hostilities that brought British and French rivalry to American soil. The control of most of the French lands on this continent—Canada and Louisiana—passed into British and Spanish hands.

Like the Spanish before them, the French left a trail of place-names across the landscape: St. Louis, Des Moines, New Orleans, Vincennes and Dubuque. But the French did not leave as lasting a series of Catholic institutions as the Spanish had in

The Ursuline convent in New Orleans, begun in 1727, is the oldest building in the city and the first convent established in the country. It is now the archbishop's residence.

the Southwest. For one reason, the French Catholic centers of settlers and Indians, unlike the mission complexes of the West, were not structured employment communities. The economy of the colonial powers in the Great Lakes and the Mississippi Valley was built around furs and trapping, not around agriculture. In addition, the intensity of French missionary activity in the New World was spent within a century, in part because of rising hostility between the French and the English. By contrast, the Spanish mission era spread over more than two hundred years.

The labors of hundreds of French clerics—Carmelites, Capuchins, Franciscans, Jesuits and Sulpicians—were, however, far from vain. Theirs was often a gentler approach to native peoples than that of their confreres to the west. It featured, for example, a stronger attempt by missionaries to learn the languages of the people. They brought lively Christian faith to thousands, and laid a groundwork for the Catholic tradition in such significant centers as New Orleans, St. Louis and Detroit.

At the time of the American Revolution, one French cleric in particular had a pivotal role. Pierre Gibault (1735-1802) settled as a young missionary at Kaskaskia, Illinois, to work among the Indians. He was responsible to the Bishop of Quebec, Joseph Briand, who had forbidden his clerics under penalty of suspension from giving any aid to the American revolutionary cause. Despite this prohibition, Gibault helped rally the citizens at Kaskaskia, Cahokia and Vincennes to the support of General George Rogers Clark, the "George Washington of the West."

For the American Revolution was not fought or won only on the east coast. The vast territory that now includes Michigan, Ohio, Indiana, Illinois and Kentucky was under British sway. When Clark was victorious in such far-flung sites as Kaskaskia and Cahokia, near St. Louis in the west or at Detroit to the north, he and his comrades helped the new nation lay claim to a vast region.

Had the fledgling nation begun with this great region at its back as a hostile force, its infant years would have been dramatically threatened. Thus Gibault's support helped Clark turn the tide of the Revolution in the west by supporting Clark's case among his congregations.

French Father Pierre Gibault, whose preaching stirred up support for the revolutionary cause in the West.

Part Two

The English Colonies: National Beginnings

A LAW
OF
MARYLAND
Concerning
RELIGION.

Oraſmuch as in awell-governed and Chriſtian Commonwealth, Matters concerning Religion and the Honour of God ought to be in the firſt plaᵗe to be taken into ſerious conſideration, and endeavoured to be ſettled. Be it therefore Ordained and Enacted by the Right Honourable CÆCILIUS Lord Baron of *Baltemore*, abſolute Lord and Proprietary of this Province, with the Advice and Conſent of the Upper and Lower Houſe of this General Aſſembly, That whatſoever perſon or perſons within this Province and the Iſlands thereunto belonging, ſhall froᵐ henceforth blaſpheme GOD, that is curſe him; or ſhall deny our Saviour JESUS CHRIST to be the Son of God; or ſhall deny the Holy Trinity, the Father, Son, & Holy Ghoſt, or the Godhead of any of the ſaid Three Perſons of the Trinity, or the Unity of the Godhead, or ſhall uſe or utter any reproachful ſpeeches, words, or language, concerning the Holy Trinity, or any of the ſaid three Perſons thereof, ſhall be puniſhed with death, and confiſcation or forfeiture of all his or her Lands and Goods to the Lord Proprietary and his Heirs.

And be it alſo enacted by the Authority, and with the advice and aſſent aforeſaid, That whatſoever perſon or perſons ſhall from henceforth uſe or utter any reproachful words or ſpeeches concerning the bleſſed Virgin *MARY*, the Mother of our Saviour, or the holy Apoſtles or Evangeliſts, or any of them, ſhall in ſuch caſe for the firſt Offence forfeit to the ſaid Lord Proprietary and his Heirs, Lords and Proprietaries of this Province, the ſum of Five pounds Sterling, or the value thereof to be levied on the goods and chattels of every ſuch perſon ſo offending; but in caſe ſuch offender or offenders ſhall not then have goods and chattels ſufficient for the ſatisfying of ſuch forfeiture, or that the ſame be not otherwiſe ſpeedily ſatisfied, that then ſuch offender or offenders ſhall be publickly whipt, and be impriſoned during the pleaſure of the Lord Proprietary, or the Lieutenant or Chief Governor of this Province for the time being: And that every ſuch offender and offenders for every ſecond offence ſhall forſeit Ten Pounds Sterling, or the value thereof to be levied as aforeſaid; or in caſe ſuch offender or offenders ſhall not then have goods and chattels within this Province ſufficient for that purpoſe, then to be publickly and ſeverely whipt and impriſoned as before is expreſſed: and that every perſon or perſons before mentioned, offending herein the third time, ſhall for ſuch third offence, forſeit all his lands and goods, and be for ever baniſht and expelled out of this Province.

And be it alſo further Enacted by the ſame Authority, advice, and aſſent, That whatſoever perſon or perſons ſhall from henceforth upon any occaſion of offence, or otherwiſe in a reproachful manner or way, declare, call, or denominate, any perſon or perſons whatſoever, inhabiting, reſiding, trafficking, trading, or commercing within this Province, or within any the Ports, Harbours, Creeks or Havens to the ſame belonging, an Heretick, Schiſmatick, Idolater, Puritan, Presbyterian, Independant, Popiſh Prieſt, Jeſuit, Jeſuited Papiſt, Lutheran, Calviniſt, Anabaptiſt, Browniſt, Barrowiſt, Antinonian, Roundhead, Separatiſt, or other name or term in a reproachfull manner relating to matter of Religion, ſhall for every ſuch offence forfeit and loſe the ſum of Ten ſhillings Sterling, or the value thereof, to be levied of the goods and chattels of every ſuch offender and offenders, the one half thereof to be forſeited and paid unto the perſon & perſons of whom ſuch reproachful words are, or ſhall be ſpoken or uttered, and the other half thereof to the Lord Proprietary and his Heirs, Lords and Proprietaries of this Province: But if ſuch perſon or perſons who ſhall at any time utter or ſpeak any ſuch reproachful words or language, ſhall not have goods or chattels ſufficient and overt within this Province to be taken to ſatiſfy the penalty aforeſaid, or that the ſame be not otherwiſe ſpeedily ſatisfied, that then the perſon and perſons ſo offending ſhall be publickly whipt, and ſhall ſuffer impriſonment without Bail or Mainpriſe untill he, ſhe, or they, reſpectively, ſhall ſatisfie the party offended or grieved by ſuch reproachfull Language, by asking him or her reſpectively forgiveneſs publickly, for ſuch his offence, before the Magiſtrate or chief Officer or Officers of the Town or place where ſuch offence ſhall be given.

And be further likewiſe enacted by the authority and conſent aforeſaid, that every perſon and perſons within this Province, that ſhall at any time hereafter prophane the Sabbath, or Lords day, called Sunday, by frequent ſwearing, drunkenneſs, or by any uncivil or diſorderly Recreation, or by working on that day when abſolute neceſſity doth not require, ſhall for every ſuch firſt offence forfeit two ſhillings ſix pence Sterling, or the value thereof; and for the ſecond offence five ſhillings Sterling, or the value thereof; and for the third offence, and for every time he ſhall offend in like manner afterwards, Ten ſhillings Sterling, or the value thereof; and in caſe ſuch offender or offenders ſhall not have ſufficient goods or chattels within this Province to ſatisfy any of the aforeſaid penalties reſpectively hereby impoſed for prophaning the Sabbath or Lords day called Sunday as aforeſaid, then in every ſuch caſe the party ſo offending ſhall for the firſt and ſecond offence in that kind be impriſoned till he or ſhe ſhall publickly in open Court before the chief Commander, Judge or Magiſtrate of that County, Town, or Precinct wherein ſuch offence ſhall be committed, acknowledge the ſcandal and offence he hath in that reſpect given, againſt God, and the good and civil Government of this Province: and for the third offence and for every time after ſhall alſo be publickly whipt.

And whereas the inforcing of the Conſcience in matter of Religion hath frequently fallen out to be of dangerous conſequence in thoſe Commonwealths where it hath been practiſed, and for the more quiet and peaceable Government of this Province, and the better to preſerve mutual love & unity amongſt the Inhabitants here, Be it therefore alſo by the Lord Proprietary with the advice and aſſent of this Aſſembly, ordained and enacted, except as in this preſent Act is before declared and ſet forth, that no perſon or perſons whatſoever within this Province, or the Iſlands, Ports, Harbors, Creeks, or Havens thereunto belonging, profeſſing to believe in Jeſus Chriſt, ſhall from henceforth be any ways troubled, moleſted, or diſcountenanced, for, or in reſpect of his or her Religion nor in the free exerciſe thereof within this Province or the Iſlands thereunto belonging, nor any way compell'd to the belief or exerciſe of any other Religion againſt his or her conſent, ſo as they be not unfaithfull to the Lord Proprietary, or moleſt or conſpire againſt the civil Government, eſtabliſhed or to be eſtabliſhed in this Province under him and his Heirs. And that all and every perſon and perſons that ſhall preſume contrary to this Act and the true intent & meaning thereof, directly or indirectly, either in perſon or eſtate, willfully to wrong, diſturb, or trouble, or moleſt any perſon or perſons whatſoever within this Province, profeſſing to believe in Jeſus Chriſt, for or in reſpect of his or her Religion, or the free exerciſe thereof within this Province, otherwiſe then is provided for in this Act, that ſuch perſon or perſons ſo offending ſhall be compelled to pay treble damages to the party ſo wronged or moleſted, and for every ſuch offence ſhall alſo forfeit Twenty ſhillings Sterling in Money, or the value there of, half thereof for the uſe of the Lord Proprietary and his Heirs, Lords and Proprietaries of this Province, and the other half thereof for the uſe of the Party ſo wronged or moleſted as aforeſaid; or if the parᵗy ſo offending as aforeſaid, ſhall refuſe or be unable to recompence the party ſo wronged, or to ſatisfy ſuch fine or forfeiture, then ſuch offender ſhall be ſeverely puniſhed by publick whipping and impriſonment during the pleaſure of the Lord Proprietary or his Lieutenant or chief Governor of this Province for the time being, without Bail or Mainpriſe.

And be it further alſo enacted by the authority and conſent aforeſaid, that tʰe Sheriff or other Officer or Officers from time to time to be appointed and authorized for that purpoſe of the County, Town, or Precinct where every particular offence in this preſent Act contained, ſhall happen at any time to be committed, and whereupon there is hereby a forfeiture, fine, or penalty impoſed, ſhall from time to time diſtrain, and ſeize the goods and eſtate of every ſuch perſon ſo offending as aforeſaid againſt this preſent Act or any part thereof, and ſell the ſame or any part thereof for the full ſatisfaction of ſuch forfeiture, fine, or penalty as aforeſaid, reſtoring to the party ſo offending, the remainder or over plus of the ſaid goods or eſtate, after ſuch ſatisfaction ſo made as aforeſaid.

Chapter Four

English Colonial Religion

The English came relatively late to the colonial enterprise in America. Under the sponsorship of Sir Walter Raleigh, a short-lived attempt to establish a colony on Roanoke Island in Virginia was made in 1585. A few families made a second attempt in 1587 but the ill-fated "Lost Colony" had disappeared without a trace by 1591. The 1607 landing at Jamestown, also in Virginia, began permanent English settlement in the colonies Britain would hold until the American Revolution.

With the arrival of the Puritans' *Mayflower* at Plymouth, Massachusetts, in 1620, the saga of intense religious activity began in English America. The first Protestant ministers arrived on the New World scene at about the same time that Spanish Catholic missions were realizing success, especially around Santa Fe in New Mexico.

By the late seventeenth century, at least four dominant groups of Christians had emerged in the British North American colonies: (1) Puritans in New England; (2) Anglicans in Virginia; (3) Quakers, Dissenters and diverse groups in Pennsylvania and the Middle Colonies; (4) Roman Catholics in Maryland.

The Toleration Act, which gave religious freedom to Maryland in 1649, was repealed by Puritans in 1654.

The Puritans who came to New England represented a movement that had begun within the Church of England in the sixteenth century. They sought to pull that tradition in a more strictly Calvinist direction, away from what they considered a theological outlook and liturgical ceremonies still too "Romish" to be appropriate to a truly Protestant Reformation.

Puritanism itself eventually divided into two streams, those who sought to work from within the Church of England to bring about change and those who instead urged separation from it in favor of a restored, pristine Christianity. Some among this last, more radical group came to be known as Pilgrims. It was a Pilgrim group who landed at Plymouth in

1620. The more moderate Puritans, under the leadership of John Winthrop, made their landfall in 1630 at Boston, establishing the Massachusetts Bay Colony. In the life of the early colonies, the distinction eventually became insignificant.

The Puritans brought with them a powerful message. They left on American life even to this day a massive mark, out of proportion to their numbers. They believed that Scripture was the sole rule of faith. That which was not sanctioned in the Bible was not to be sanctioned at all. Accordingly, their churches were usually plain white meetinghouses, lacking stained glass or statues. At the sanctuary's center stood the pulpit, where the minister might orate literally for hours on end. Today such churches appear not only on the New England landscape, but also as an American archetype on countless calendars and Christmas cards.

The Pilgrims at Sunday worship in Plymouth.

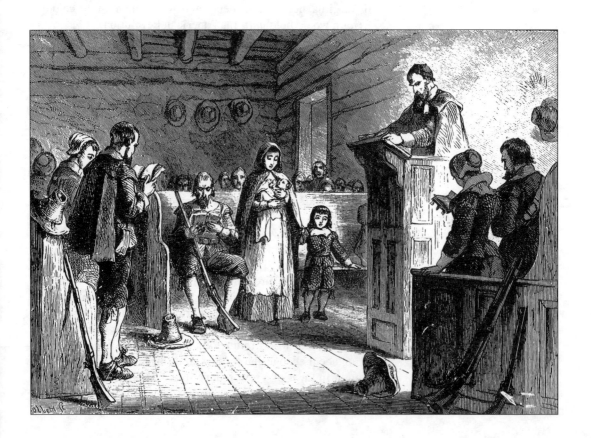

For Discussion

What echoes of the Puritan work ethic do you hear in political arguments today? What traces of their sense of special destiny can still be seen in American international policies?

Additionally, the Puritans held a stern view of predestination. Individuals chosen by God should be able to give evidence of such election. Success in one's worldly vocation was interpreted as one such sign, and as a result, Puritans highly valued hard work and industry—the origins of the well-known "Puritan work ethic."

Church and State should be joined together for the common good, these stern believers maintained, with the Church as the dominant partner. Only those who showed evidence of being chosen by God were permitted to participate in community affairs. Even so, a democratic system of selecting leaders, based on models in the biblical book of the Acts of the Apostles, was allowed, giving birth to the famous New England town meeting with its bow to popular government. Once the elected officer was in place, however, he became in modern parlance a very strong executive.

Because the Puritans insisted over and over again on the absolute authority of God alone, they left a kind of loophole in their theory of state for the overthrow of a wicked or ungodly king. Some historians have seen in this proviso an early stepping-stone toward the revolution that toppled George III from his rule of the colonies.

Because the Bible was central in Puritan lives, they demanded careful education of the ministers who led the people in scriptural paths. To this end, Harvard was established in 1636, the first major school in the English colonies. Since all people were to be familiar with the Scriptures, New England leaders also tried to provide early education for all children (especially boys, with an occasional "dame school" for colonial girls).

To the Puritans, then, has rightly gone at least partial credit for many of America's foundational tenets: education, hard work, democratic systems and the maintenance of biblically based moral standards.

But one pillar of our society these Calvinists did not erect: toleration. The Puritans came to the American shores seeking religious freedom for themselves alone. Those who dissented from accepted belief and practice (such as Anne Hutchinson and Roger Williams in the 1630's) were cast out of the colony. More difficult individuals suffered public whipping, even death. Mary Dyer "did hang like a flag" on Boston Common on June 1, 1660, for preaching Quakerism and defying banishment

The Puritan Vision

Now the only way to avoid shipwreck and to provide for our posterity is to follow the counsel of Micah (6:8): to do justly, to love mercy, and to walk humbly with our God. For this end, we must be knit together in this work as one.... We must entertain one another in...affection; we must be willing to abridge ourselves of our superfluities, for the supply of others' necessities....

We must delight in each other, make others' conditions our own, rejoice together, mourn together, labor and suffer together....

So shall we keep the unity of the spirit in the bond of peace....

We shall find that the God of Israel is among us, when ten of us shall resist a thousand of our enemies, when He shall make us a promise and a glory, that men may say of succeeding plantations, "The Lord make it like that of New England." For we must consider that we shall be a city set upon a hill, the eyes of all people are upon us. (From John Winthrop's Sermon on Board the *Arbella*, 1630.

decrees. (Her execution seared the conscience of the Puritans' latter-day descendants, who erected a statue of the Quaker martyr that stands in downtown Boston today.) Even more drastically, Puritan leaders at Salem, Massachusetts in 1692 imprisoned over one hundred fifty individuals and hung nineteen women for supposed witchcraft.

The Puritans' intolerance and intensity was born in part out of the one pervasive characteristic they were to bequeath to the United States for good and for ill: a sense of special destiny. In the famous sermon John Winthrop preached on board the *Arbella* as it sailed into Massachusetts Bay in 1630, he maintained that this small and hardy band of religious adventurers were establishing a "city set upon a hill" for all the world to watch and imitate. This first statement of the theme of "manifest destiny" echoes throughout American history, surfacing not only in the theological realm, but the political, economic and military as well.

Some Puritan values were officially rejected by the new nation: the union of Church and State, the intolerance of other faiths. But many others—education, special destiny, relentless work, democratic structures—remained, subtly establishing national expectations and goals. When Catholics began flooding into the United States in the nineteenth century, they would find an unwritten, modified Puritan ethos already in place.

Of all the things the Puritans feared, the Roman Catholic Church stood next to Satan himself. Jonathan Edwards, one of the most eloquent Puritan divines, maintained that God had kept the new land hidden from European discovery until after the Reformation had taken place. The way was thus opened for authentic Christianity, free of the excess Edwards perceived in Roman Catholic ritual, doctrine and—most especially—hierarchical structure.

Anti-Catholicism came early to the colonies and stayed late. In Europe the fury of the Reformation still animated Protestants and Catholics alike, and resulted not only in intolerance, but often in violence. In the English colonies of America, Catholics were a very small minority. By 1700 Catholic numbers in Maryland, by far the largest center of colonial Catholic concentration, stood at only about two thousand, five hundred—not an unlikely population for a suburban American parish today.

When Puritans seized control of England in the 1640's, life for the few colonial Catholics in America became more restrictive and dangerous. A Massachusetts statute of 1647 threatened with death any priest who persisted in remaining within its borders. And after the "Glorious Revolution" of 1688 replaced Catholic James II with William and Mary on the throne of England, Catholics frequently had the added burden of supporting an established Church of England with their taxes.

In New England, as the eighteenth century advanced, Puritan dominance faded. The Church of England increased in power and prestige and the Baptist, Methodist and Presbyterian Churches grew significantly. But the Catholic minority still remained second-class citizens. Except at St. Joseph's Church, founded at Philadelphia in 1733, they were not generally permitted to worship in public. Among other civil inequities, by the eve of the American Revolution, Catholics were prohibited from voting or holding office in many colonies.

A second model of early colonial Christianity was Anglican Virginia. Shortly after the foundation of Jamestown in 1607, an attempt was made to establish the Church of England in the colony. But the fact that the area's economy was built on scattered plantations held dim promise for a tradition built on village church parishes. This did not thwart a very early though short-lived attempt to enforce religious and moral practice in Virginia. Under Dale's Laws of 1611, those who failed to worship daily in the church could be fined or whipped; repeated blasphemers were subject to execution.

A third style of Church government in early America was established in Pennsylvania—Penn's Woods—established by Quaker William Penn in 1681. Here, wide toleration was practiced in religious matters, and the colony soon became a haven for those persecuted for their faith. Even today, Pennsylvania is widely populated by such groups as the Amish and Hutterites, whose ancestors were hounded from their native lands. William Penn (1644-1718) became widely known not only for his religious toleration, but also for his rare sense of the need to render justice to the American Indian. Here, truly, was a man morally ahead of his age.

The Maryland colony was the most unusual because it was founded by the Catholic Sir George Calvert, Lord Baltimore (1580-1632) at a time when Catholics by and large suffered all manner of legal restrictions in England. Upon Calvert's death, his eldest son Cecil (1606-1675) became the proprietor of the Maryland colony, named to honor Queen Henrietta Marie, wife of King Charles I.

An Oxford graduate, Cecil, the second Lord Baltimore, commissioned his brother Leonard as governor of Maryland's first settlers. Aboard the ships *Ark* and *Dove*, sometimes called the Catholic *Mayflowers*, this religiously diverse group (predominantly Protestant) left England in November, 1633, arriving on St. Clement's Island, Maryland, on March 25, 1634. Jesuit Andrew White celebrated the colony's first Mass that day.

Contrary to some misconceptions, the majority of Maryland's population was never Catholic. Yet members of the ancient faith were not only substantially represented in Maryland, they also held much wealth and social status. Three Jesuits—two priests and a brother—crossed in the founding

For Discussion

Compare the religious tolerance of English Catholic colonists to the zeal for converts exhibited by the Spanish and French. What social and historical factors may account for the difference?

Quaker William Penn (left), founder of Pennsylvania, and the Catholic Lords Baltimore, Sir George Calvert (center) and Sir Cecil Calvert (right), proprietors of the Maryland colony.

voyage of 1634, and at the town of St. Mary's established the first formal Catholic religious house in English America.

Before their departure for the New World, the second Lord Baltimore carefully instructed those sailing to his colony in the way of religious interaction. According to James Hennesey in *American Catholics*, all "acts of Roman Catholique religion" were to be "done as privately as may be." And Catholics were told to be "silent on all occasions of discourse concerning matters of religion." In short, they were to keep a very low religious profile.

Thus began the first "Catholic colony" on the Eastern seaboard. Its establishment reflected many motives: political and economic betterment as well as religious freedom. From the beginning the Catholic leadership espoused a policy of religious liberty. The Maryland Act of Toleration, passed in 1649, gave the informal arrangement the force of law.

A generation before Penn's "Holy Experiment" in Pennsylvania, Catholics became the first English colonists to establish a community broadly ecumenical (for its day), granting religious freedom to all Christians. Was such an act a mere expedient, intended only to safeguard a powerful minority? Historians have argued the point for centuries. These early Catholic leaders were of an educated class that had survived a century of persecution. Unlike the first Spanish and French Catholics, who had come to the New Land with their hearts set on conversion, they showed no tendency to proselytize, no zeal to convert their neighbors. Of practical temperament, they appreciated religious toleration for what it is: a sensible way for diverse groups to live together.

As Father Hennesey noted in *American Catholics*, even a frequent critic of Catholicism such as historian Robert Baird had granted the significance of Maryland toleration: ..."[We] cannot refuse to Lord Baltimore's colony the praise of having established the first government in modern times in which entire toleration was granted to all denominations of Christians."

Maryland Catholics were not to enjoy their newfound freedom for long. As Oliver Cromwell's Puritans seized power in England's Civil War (1642-1648), a Puritan party took control in Maryland as well. They repealed the Act of Toleration in 1654. Then began a terrible repression that saw four executions, the expulsion of priests and the seizure of

St. Joseph's Parish, founded in Philadelphia in 1733, according to a 1776 picture.

lands that belonged to the Jesuits.

Lord Baltimore's party returned to power for a few years, but in 1691 Maryland became a royal colony, and the Church of England became the established Church the following year. For nearly a century to follow, Catholics were denied public worship, the vote and their own schools.

Nevertheless, the repression of Catholics in their flagship colony was neither constant nor unrelenting. The faithful managed to worship in private. One of the most powerful landowners in Maryland in the seventeenth century was a Catholic: Margaret Brent (1601-1671). Many of the wealthy "first families" of Maryland were Catholic, including the Brookes, Neales and, of course, the Carrolls, a dynasty that produced major players in the saga of the new American Republic.

The Jesuits, who had opened a school at Newtown Manor in 1653 (the first such institution in the American English colonies) operated another, Bohemia Manor, in the 1740's along Chesapeake Bay. Additionally, the Jesuits maintained their slave-worked plantations, whose profits helped to keep Jesuit missions afloat. (Slavery was not unusual in religious houses. John Carroll, America's first bishop, was a slaveholder, as were other bishops and religious communities, as we will see in Chapter Eight.)

The simple fact is that Catholics, despite restrictive legislation, managed to outwit much official intolerance—at times, because of loose enforcement.

By the Revolution, the twenty-five thousand Catholics in the colonies were less than one percent of the total population. Even so, their numbers had increased tenfold in seventy-five years, augmented in particular by black slaves (perhaps twenty percent of the Maryland Catholic population) and Irish immigrants.

The largest concentrations of Catholics at the end of the colonial era were in the rural counties of St. Mary's and Charles, Maryland, and at St. Joseph parish in Philadelphia, a congregation that numbered Irish, English and Germans among its parishioners.

By the 1740's, a pair of German priests served the scattered Catholics of their nationality settling in the Susquehanna, Schuylkill and Delaware Valleys. New York City by 1776 was visited periodically by German Jesuit Father Ferdinand Farmer,

For Discussion

What countries today maintain an established religion? How does that concept impact the daily lives of their citizens?

Irish Catholic Thomas Dongan, governor of New York City from 1683 to 1688, established religious freedom for Catholics, Protestants and Jews.

who offered Mass secretly for the few Catholics there in a loft in present-day lower Manhattan. A brief period in the mid-seventeenth century saw modest Catholic growth in the city. Irish Catholic Thomas Dongan served as governor from 1683 to 1688, his term ending abruptly about the time the Glorious Revolution brought William and Mary to power in the motherland. Anti-Catholic sentiment forced Dongan to flee the area.

While in office, Dongan was responsible for a "Charter of Libertys and Privileges" that established religious freedom as state policy. By his action as well, early Jews in New York were granted greater liberties and civic opportunities. "Thus," wrote John Tracy Ellis, dean of American Catholic historians, in *American Catholicism*, "did New York's Catholic governor join the honorable company of Roger Williams, Lord Baltimore and William Penn as the chief promoters of religious freedom in colonial America."

From the settlement of America until the end of the colonial period, Catholics in English America were served by some one hundred Jesuit priests, as well as by six Franciscans. Their piety was nurtured, in addition, by prayer manuals that had served English Catholics through the long years when their clergy were banished. Most prominent among such books was Richard Challoner's *The Garden of the Soul*, published in 1740. It emphasized internal, personal piety rather than public worship. The importance of the eucharistic presence within each believer was stressed, along with the need for lay Catholics to be involved in the tasks and professions around them.

In summary, Catholics in colonial America represented a minuscule portion of the population. They tended to keep a very low profile throughout the colonial era, as if in strict obedience to the admonition of Lord Baltimore in 1633. They made no large-scale attempt to convert their fellow citizens, but were among the first Catholics in the world to champion the cause of religious toleration and liberty in matters of Church and State. It was especially appropriate that the document dubbed the "American gift" at the Second Vatican Council— the *Declaration on Religious Liberty*—should have come mainly from the heart and hand of a Maryland-based Jesuit: John Courtney Murray.

These colonial Catholics maintained fidelity to their

religion, even though the general tenor of place and time was decidedly anti-Catholic. They would be startled by an American nation in which Catholicism is not only an accepted part of the mainstream, but also the largest single denomination.

Paul pinx.   Lovelace Sculp.

The Right Rev. John

BISHOP OF BALTIMORE.

Publish'd as the Act directs, Nov. 6th 1790, by J. P. Coghlan, Duke Street, Grosvenor Square, London.

Chapter Five

Twin Revolutions

As the fateful year of independence drew near, the English colonists of North America numbered some two and a half million people; nearly one-fourth of these were people of color, most of them slaves. The three largest cities had smaller populations than many modern suburbs: an estimated thirty thousand in Philadelphia, twenty-five thousand in New York City and sixteen thousand in Boston.

The religious statistics of the era are even more startling. Although numbers, based on some historical surmise, are not precise, it is estimated that no more than ten percent of the people were members of any particular Church by the time of Washington's first presidential term in the 1790's. The churchgoing fraction belonged, for the most part, to the following denominations: New England Congregational (the largest, with seven hundred fifty congregations), Presbyterian, Baptist, Anglican, Quaker and Lutheran (the smallest, with two hundred forty congregations).

Bishop John Carroll, the first bishop of the primal see, Baltimore.

Many of these Churches had realized a windfall of new members as a result of the famous "Great Awakening" of the 1740's, a revival movement inspired by the intense preaching of such luminaries as Jonathan Edwards and George Whitfield. Even though this movement pushed the religious population beyond ten percent, the figures pale in comparison with the fifty to sixty percent church membership of the mid-twentieth century. The modern mythology that portrays the early United States as a profoundly churchgoing society cannot stand the test of historical scrutiny.

How do historians account for the relatively large percentage of unchurched citizens? The reasons are many: The population was widely scattered, not clustered in traditional parish or congregational patterns. The earliest colonists (Puritans excepted) more often gave economic matters priority

47

over theological ones. Religion in the homelands was declining in reaction to religious bickering and wars. Additionally, the new Enlightenment thinkers placed a higher value on rational religion than on traditional Christianity.

The Enlightenment took the intellectuals of eighteenth-century Europe by storm. Fueled by the writings of John Locke in England, Diderot and Voltaire in France and Kant in Germany, some espoused a deist theology, which emphasized only those tenets of religion that reason alone could discover. Many came to value questioning over acceptance and authority, reason over revelation and historical tradition, and an optimistic view of humanity over a sinful, pessimistic one.

The Enlightenment spirit would, of course, cross the ocean, animating the work of Thomas Paine, Benjamin Franklin and Thomas Jefferson. Nowhere did the new rationalist spirit find more concise or dramatic expression than in Jefferson's Declaration of Independence with its invocation of nature's God and inalienable rights. While the Enlightenment represented a thought current among intellectuals rather than a popular religious movement, it would profoundly influence the leaders of the new nation.

When the young republic proudly placed the words *Novus Ordo Seclorum*—The New Order of the Ages—on its seal, it proclaimed the Enlightenment creed for all to see. (To this day, the seal with its motto appears on the back of every dollar bill.) Two streams, the Puritan concept of special destiny and the Enlightenment confidence in a new world of rational perfectibility, flowed together in the mainstream of American thought. This union was the unlikeliest of marriages. Nearly diametrically opposed in every other way, these two ideologies shared the common conviction that America should model and proclaim to the world a new order of the ages. This was a bold cry to arise from an infant, powerless nation. And it proved a persistent theme, shaping the economic, military and international politics of the nation ever after.

Within this diverse blend of Enlightened and Quaker, Puritan and Presbyterian, churched and unchurched, Roman Catholics continued to represent a tradition that many colonists considered an alien, even dangerous force. Massachusetts patriot Sam Adams concluded that freedom was more threatened by the growth of "popery" in America than from the passage of the Stamp Act by the British Parliament. The great

The Great Seal of the United States.

For Discussion

During the Enlightenment, which influenced such key leaders as Benjamin Franklin, Thomas Jefferson and Thomas Paine, advances in science and technology spawned new faith in human progress and problem-solving ability. In what areas of modern American life is this philosophy still apparent?

irony, of course, is that the Catholics of the colonies constituted at most one percent of the population. When the Revolution began, New York City, Boston and Charleston had not a single permanent Catholic parish within their boundaries. There may have been fewer than six hundred Catholics in all New England.

And yet many Catholics played a significant role in the achievement of American independence. Adherents of the ancient faith had little love for the British, who had long oppressed them both in England and in America. An independent country that granted true toleration to all faiths would be decidedly to their own advantage.

In Maryland, Catholic Charles Carroll of Carrollton (1737-1832), writing as "First Citizen" in the *America Gazette*, challenged the British power to tax without representation as early as 1773. The next year Carroll carried his convictions with him to the Continental Congress. He wielded deciding influence at Annapolis, the seat of the colonial government, when Maryland cast its lot with the revolutionary cause in 1776. And as a delegate to the 1776 Continental Congress at Philadelphia, Charles Carroll became the sole Catholic signer of the Declaration of Independence.

Although he was not a delegate at Philadelphia, Pennsylvania Catholic Thomas Fitzsimons (1741-1811) labored for independence within his state's convention, and later would organize a company of militia, serving with distinction as a captain during the Revolutionary War. Other prominent Catholic Philadelphians who rendered high service to the patriot cause were General Stephen Moylan (1734-1811), aide to General Washington, and Navy Commodore John Barry (1754-1803). Large numbers of Catholic recruits from St. Mary's County served with distinction in Maryland's Old Line Company.

In the critical year of 1776, Charles Carroll and his cousin John traveled to Canada with Benjamin Franklin and Samuel Chase in an attempt to win northern sympathy for the American cause. The presence of the two Catholics was far from accidental; to the Canadians, with their considerable French Catholic population, the very presence of their fellow religionists in the delegation spoke mightily.

Eager Catholic support for the revolution was not limited to the masculine gender. In Pennsylvania, Sara McCalla nursed the wounded at the Battle of Brandywine. Maryland's Mary Digges Lee organized the support of other women around the revolutionaries and later would receive General Washington's plaudits for her efforts. The Philadelphia "doctoress" Mary Wateus offered her services in military hospitals during the conflict.

In faraway Arizona, the Spanish, no friends to the British Empire, followed events along the Atlantic seaboard with great interest. It is hardly surprising to discover that many Spanish missionaries pledged not only their prayers but also their pesos to the colonists. In California Father Junipero Serra sent a letter to his clerical colleagues, urging them to pray that God would grant success to the cause. Along the Mississippi, as we saw in Chapter Three, Father Pierre Gibault used his influence to win the support of his coreligionists for General George Rogers Clark.

After the revolution, old animosities began to diminish in many (though not all) quarters, only to resurface with a vengeance in later generations. In New York, the anti-priest statute was erased from the law books as early as 1784.

The choice of a leader of the Catholic faithful in the new nation was not difficult. John Carroll (1735-1815) had emerged as a promising public-spirited clergyman in early 1776 when he accompanied his cousin Charles Carroll and Benjamin Franklin on their diplomatic mission to Canada. It was Franklin who, in response to the inquiry of the papal nuncio in Paris in 1784, recommended Carroll's appointment as the first head of the American Catholic Church.

Carroll was himself born into a Maryland family of social and financial substance. Young John received most of his higher education in Flanders and France. In 1753, he entered the Jesuit order, serving as tutor and teacher in Europe until his return to Maryland in 1774. It is likely that in these years the future Bishop Carroll drank in some of the Enlightenment ideals that would underlie his early years in the Baltimore diocese.

From 1784 to 1789, Carroll served as "Superior of the Missions." Throughout the 80's, as in an article in the *United States Gazette* in June 1789, he argued for religious freedom for all citizens and for a nation built on "the soundest principles of justice and equal liberty."

When the Constitution transformed the loose confederation

For Discussion

Enlightenment thinkers generally lumped religion with superstition. Discuss the difference.

Carroll Prays for the Government—1800

We pray thee, O God of might, wisdom and justice, through whom laws are enacted and judgment decreed, assist with Thy Holy Spirit of counsel and fortitude the President of these United States, that his administration may be conducted in righteousness and be eminently useful to Thy people over whom he presides by encouraging due respect for virtue and religion; by a faithful execution of the laws in justice and mercy; and by restraining vice and immorality.

Let the light of Thy divine wisdom direct the proceedings and laws framed for our rule and government, so that they may tend to the preservation of peace, the promotion of national happiness, an increase in industry, sobriety and useful knowledge; and may perpetuate to us the blessings of equal liberty. (From *Documents of American Catholic History*, edited by John Tracy Ellis)

of colonies into the United States of America in 1789, Rome decided that the Church in the republic was entitled to full diocesan status. Accordingly, the clergy of the infant country were invited to select the man who would serve as the first American bishop. The choice was not surprising. At Whitemarsh Plantation, Maryland, in May 1789, the assembled priests chose John Carroll as bishop of Baltimore. The diocese he was to administer comprised the entire new nation, stretching from the Atlantic to the Mississippi and from the Great Lakes to the Florida border.

Before the new bishop could assume his post, a small problem immediately needed tending: In order for a bishop to be consecrated, other bishops must be present to lay their hands on his head in the ancient ceremonies. But no bishops were to be found in America, only some twenty-five priests. (Most were former Jesuits. They were still priests in good standing, but the order itself was suppressed by the pope in 1773 due to political pressures in Europe. It not fully restored until 1814.)

Accordingly, John Carroll set sail for England, where he was consecrated bishop with full ceremony at Lulworth Castle on the Feast of the Assumption, August 15, 1790.

John Carroll was an American profoundly attuned to the political and philosophic dynamic of his country. A gentleman of old Maryland stock who believed deeply in wide religious freedom, he also was an early supporter of the election of bishops by the priests of a diocese, as well as the use of the vernacular in liturgy.

But just as the revolutionary nation gave way to a conservative, aristocratic era under the Federalist presidents George Washington and John Adams, John Carroll in his new role of authority became increasingly cautious about a democracy in the inner life of the Church. In part, Carroll and other democratic leaders were frightened in the 1790's by such excesses of the French Revolution as the mass execution of the nobility, priests and nuns, and the conversion of Notre Dame Cathedral into a "Temple of Reason."

When the European immigrants, accustomed to more traditional, centralized authority poured into America later in the nineteenth century, the stage would be set for a Church that more readily followed European patterns of polity and piety. Still, even in Bishop Carroll's more conservative phase, his Prayer for the Government (see page 51) brimmed with words dear to Jefferson: *national happiness*, *useful knowledge*, *equal liberty*.

Meanwhile in Baltimore (and radiating from it as from a capital city) the Catholic institutional culture began to emerge. French Sulpician priests, first contacted by Carroll on his consecration journey, arrived in Baltimore in 1791 to begin St. Mary's Seminary, the first school in the nation for the education of priests. The French fathers maintained a college in Baltimore (also called St. Mary's) for a half century after 1799; they also established Mount St. Mary's College in Emmitsburg, Maryland, in 1808. St. Mary's Seminary and Mount St. Mary's continue still as major centers of theological education.

In 1790, Bishop Carroll welcomed into his diocese its first community of nuns, the Discalced Carmelites from Antwerp. When this contemplative group settled at Port Tobacco in Maryland, they were the only community of women religious in the United States. Ursuline sisters had been at New Orleans since 1727, but that southern enclave of Catholicism was still under Spanish control and would be named a diocese in its own right in 1793.

In the area that became the new national capital at Washington, Bishop Carroll saw to the founding of what is now the country's oldest Catholic university: "the Academy of Georgetown, Patowmack River, Maryland." Shortly after the Jesuits were partially restored, in 1805, Georgetown came under their auspices. Close by, another significant first appeared: the establishment by the Sisters of the Visitation of a Catholic academy for girls—Visitation—in 1799.

Outside the Baltimore area, the Catholic Church began to take root in such larger cities as Boston and New York in the 1780's. But these foundations were often stormy and troubled. The first resident priest in New York, Capuchin Charles Whelan, a Revolutionary naval chaplain, disedified many of his parishioners by his tough manners and inability to preach. When a second Capuchin, Andrew Nugent, appeared on the scene, the two clerics found themselves in contention for control of the parish. Nugent took charge of the church, but was later dismissed by Carroll for misbehavior. Questions of authority and control were very lively in early American

One Mile House in Baltimore, which in 1791 became the home of St. Mary's, the first Catholic seminary in the new country.

Catholicism. They erupted again in the early nineteenth century in the uproar over trusteeism (see pp. 61-64, Chapter Six).

Partly because of financial difficulties, Boston's first resident Catholic cleric, Claude de la Poterie, would also find himself suspended by Bishop Carroll. Another early controversial priest in Boston was the outspoken John Thayer, a convert from Unitarianism who had attended Yale College. Considered temperamentally unsuitable for his Boston posting, Thayer moved on to other American missions, where his open abolitionism made for further discontent. Philadelphia boasted at this time a small but thriving Catholic community. Among its members was publisher Matthew Carey (1760-1839), who was responsible for the first American printing of a Catholic version of the Bible, later known as "the Carey Bible."

By the 1780's, the frontier was already beckoning to Americans. One of the first priests to serve pioneer Catholics in western Pennsylvania was the colorful and morally stern Russian Prince Dimitri Gallitzin (1770-1840). The first priest

The Basilica of the Assumption (the "old cathedral") in Baltimore, dedicated in 1821, was designed by Benjamin H. Latrobe, one of the architects of the U.S. Capitol.

The Cathedral, Baltimore.

to be ordained in the United States (in 1793), Stephen Badin (1768-1853) went to Kentucky at the order of Bishop Carroll. There the twenty-six-year-old exile from the French Revolution served a scattered flock whose previous priests had been short-lived in their ministries—in part because of quarrels over clerical salaries.

In the post-revolutionary era Catholics, together with adherents of all the major Churches, puzzled over what relationship the new Republic should establish with such diverse religious groups. The answer was in the Bill of Rights, enacted in 1791 as the first ten amendments to the Constitution. Under the provisions of the First Amendment, two principles were firmly established: (1) the nation would have no established (tax-supported) religion; (2) free exercise of religion was to be safeguarded for all citizens.

This separation of Church and State, so familiar to us, was considered risky—even shocking—to many Europeans of the age. Since the fourth-century establishment of Christianity in the Roman Empire, the nearly unquestioned wisdom had insisted that, however uneasy the alliance, Church and State must remain locked together in solidarity for the public good. From the view of the Church, such an arrangement provided not only financial support, but also the force of law for the dictates of Judeo-Christian morality. From the state's perspective, a single Church, united in worship and dogma, constituted the best kind of preventive medicine for society, for such a Church served to bring a sense of unity to a people as well as inculcating moral teaching and sanctions. Put bluntly, the more persuasive the moral preachers who could turn their hearers away from evil, the fewer police needed to stamp out crime. Even the Reformation of the sixteenth century did not change the insistence on such a linkage, as Protestant and Catholic rulers alike carved out territories of religious influence. Northern Germany became largely Lutheran; Geneva, Calvinist; England, Anglican; while France, Spain and Italy remained Catholic.

But with the American initiative of 1791, a new order truly dawned in religious affairs. For the first time since the early Middle Ages, a western nation had declared separation of Church and State official policy. As American life has proved, the separation was pretty friendly. Even though institutional Church and State were disjointed, religion and government

Father Stephen Badin, first priest ordained in the United States, served Catholics in Kentucky.

never went completely separate ways. There are many signs that the founding heritage of the colonies never completely departed the land: tax exemption of Church properties, chaplains in the military and in legislatures, the invocation of God on the coinage and the semi-religious holidays of Thanksgiving and Christmas.

And yet, a major change of direction clearly took place. Churches in America entered into a system akin to a theological free market. No longer braced by state support, moral or financial, the Churches had to appeal to citizens on the basis of their own persuasiveness and attractiveness. In addition, the familiar role of the Churches in Europe as nearly automatic defenders of state policy was at an end. The path was opened, even if not by direct design, for the religious traditions to raise critical voices. Later American history is replete with examples of religious leaders who assumed a prophetic role, challenging national laws and practice—issues from slavery to war, from abortion to civil rights.

Catholics played no small part in bringing to birth the American religious experiment in the separation of Church and State. They were, throughout their history, to pay its price and reap its benefits. Small wonder that their first bishop, John Carroll, could write: "...in these United States our religious system has undergone a revolution, if possible, more extraordinary than our political one."

Opposite page: Anti-Catholic cartoon protesting Rome's decision to raise the new nation to diocesan status and appoint a bishop to head it.

Chapter Six

Moving West

In the two generations after the establishment of the Diocese of Baltimore in 1789, the Catholic Church in the new country maintained its low profile. In 1808 Pope Pius VII had recognized the slow but steady growth of the Church in the land by establishing four new dioceses: Boston, New York, Philadelphia and Bardstown, Kentucky; at the same time Baltimore was raised to the status of an archdiocese. Numbers remained relatively small—some two percent of the population in 1820.

Few Catholics were national household names in America—even in Catholic households. Those whom later history would revere were known by comparatively small groups. One such was former slave Pierre Toussaint (1766-1853) who became noted in New York City for his piety, humor and constant generosity to the sick and the poor. Deeply devoted to his wife and family, Toussaint nursed the poor during epidemics, opened his home to homeless youth and walked daily to Mass in an era when the use of horses was denied to blacks in New York City. (Rome is currently investigating him as a possible candidate for sainthood.)

Catholic Sioux Indians in a South Dakota Mission served by Benedictine priests.

Better known in wider Catholic circles was the redoubtable Elizabeth Bayley Seton (1774-1821), the first American-born canonized saint. A daughter of the distinguished colonial Bayley family and wife of wealthy merchant William Seton, Elizabeth was the mother of five children. Widowed at 30, she converted to Catholicism in 1805. In 1808, she moved to Baltimore, establishing both a school for girls and the nucleus of the Sisters of Charity. The following year she moved to Emmitsburg in western Maryland, where she also laid the groundwork for what was to become the parochial school system.

Elizabeth Seton was a tireless individual, possessed of a

Right: St. Elizabeth Ann Seton, founder of the Sisters of Charity, laid the groundwork for the parochial school system. Opposite: St. Joseph's Academy, founded in 1809 by Elizabeth Seton near Emmitsburg in western Maryland, as it looked in 1829.

spirit both critical and kindly. She labored as writer and teacher, nurse and administrator. Her growing community of sisters staffed schools and orphanages as well, all under her competent leadership.

This was an era when Church leadership, according to historian James Kenneally, tended to look upon the ideal woman as frail, delicate and in need of constant protection. Elizabeth Seton broke the mold. At times she quarreled mightily with her male religious superiors, and was nearly expelled from her own congregation. "Rules..., subjection," Seton once wrote, were "dreadful walls to a burning soul as wild as mine."

She kept within such walls, however, finding ultimate value in the system. But she learned to be a consistent critic as well. To a new priest who had delivered a poor sermon at Mount St. Mary's in 1815, she scolded: "O Sir! That awakens my anger. Do you remember that a priest holds the honor of God on his lips? Do you not trouble yourself to spread His fire? ...If you will not study and prepare while young, what when you are old?"

Throughout these early nineteenth-century years, American Catholics were busy at the work of *consolidating* into new urban parishes in the East, and at *expanding* of the faith into the new frontiers of the West. It was largely in the eastern cities that the revolutionary spirit in religion foreseen by Bishop Carroll (see page 57) began to make itself manifest.

One of the most vexing problems of his administration (1789-1815)—indeed, one that would trouble the American Church until the Civil War—clustered around the phenomenon that came to be known as "trusteeism." The term means that, following American legal precedent, church congregations elected a board of trustees who were responsible for the disposition of church property as well as the selection (and

even dismissal) of pastors.

Wealthy patrons had exercised such control in some European situations. But the American spin was the republican spirit of the new nation, which opened up the prospect of congregations exercising such authority.

From a positive point of view, this meant that congregations, through their elected trustees, were directly involved in the life of their communities. They could function with their spiritual leaders as (in the later terminology of the Second Vatican Council) "the people of God." They could prove to their Protestant neighbors that they were not "clergy-ridden," a frequent charge made against Catholic immigrants.

But trusteeism had a shadow side as well. European situations in which powerful laypeople had been allowed to dominate Church affairs had often proved prescriptions for serious difficulty, if not disaster. As historian Patrick Carey puts it, "Lay intervention in pastoral appointments represented the worst kind of tyranny, made pastors slaves of congregational whim and at times imprisoned the preaching of the Gospel."

The issue of trusteeism surfaced frequently in antebellum Catholicism. While large number of parishes were never involved in disputes, the battles between parishioners and between groups of parishioners and the bishop often festered for years. The central sticking points were two questions: Who should hold title to Church property? And who should appoint the pastor? By the advent of the Civil War, the answer was clear: the bishop. Bishops were able to gain control over both material matters and the selection of clerical leaders, according to historian Carey, "through individual efforts, conciliar legislation, papal support and new American laws."

Not until the era of the Second Vatican Council ushered in such structures as parish councils and diocesan pastoral councils was the Church in the United States ready to attempt again a significant role for lay leadership. Even then, while laity were involved in making decisions about pastoral and financial priorities, property titles and clerical appointments remained firmly in the bishops' hands.

Trusteeism first found a voice at New York City's oldest parish, St. Peter's, in 1785. Philadelphia was long convulsed by disputes, the first occurring at Holy Trinity, a primarily

For Discussion

One problem area in trusteeism was parishes' insistence on choosing their own pastors. Suppose your parish council could hire or fire a pastor: What advantages or disadvantages would the practice have?

German congregation—the first "national" parish in the country. When the parishioners refused to accept the appointment of a priest by Bishop Carroll, the resulting schism lasted from 1796 to 1802. In the same City of Brotherly Love, St. Mary's Cathedral witnessed in the 1820's a revolt led by Father William Hogan, who accepted the principles of trusteeism. Rallies and elections were held, a small riot broke out, and the bishop for a time was barred from the church.

In New Orleans (part of American jurisdiction after the 1803 Louisiana Purchase), there was trouble when the *marguilliers* ("churchwardens") of St. Louis Cathedral supported New Orleans' troublesome "Père Antoine," Antonio de Sedella, over the pastor assigned by Bishop Carroll. Other outbreaks of trustee assertiveness were to occur in Charleston, Norfolk and Buffalo. The problems of trusteeism, in fact, likely hastened the creation of new dioceses, such as Charleston and Richmond in 1820, so that bishops could be physically closer to battling congregations.

In the Irish-born first bishop of Charleston, John England (1786-1842), the Church in America found a more democratic brand of leadership. England, sensing both the strengths and weaknesses in trusteeism, quickly moved to forestall conflicts by establishing an early version of a diocesan council, on which laity and clergy sat. The Irish-born prelate, with the editorial assistance of his sister Joanna England (1800-1827), founded the *United States Catholic Miscellany* as America's first Catholic newspaper in 1822. In 1826, England's reputation and oratorical skills earned him an invitation to speak before Congress in Washington. This he accomplished with great aplomb: Dressed in full pontifical attire, he lectured the nation's lawmakers for over two hours.

Bishop John England, the Irish-born first bishop of Charleston, brought a democratic leadership style to the American Church.

As the number of bishops in America grew, their periodic gatherings at Baltimore, the first see, assumed greater importance. Until the late 1840's, when other archdioceses were established by Rome, all the United States dioceses were within the jurisdiction of Baltimore. For this reason, the first seven bishops' meetings at Baltimore (1829, 1833, 1837, 1840, 1843, 1846, 1849) were called *provincial* councils (meetings of the province of Baltimore). The three held later in the century (1852, 1866, 1884) are *plenary* councils (including *all* archbishops and bishops).

From the first meeting in 1829, ethnic tension was in the

air. Baltimore's French-born Archbishop Ambrose Maréchal had not been convinced of the need for such a meeting, and resisted Bishop England's repeated call for one. In part, Maréchal feared the growing power of the Irish in the American Church, and was not eager to give the Charleston bishop, with all his Cork eloquence, a platform. Only when English-born James Whitfield succeeded Maréchal as Archbishop of Baltimore was the council finally called.

The legislation of the 1829 assembly signals the problems and priorities of the Church of that age. The bishops enacted regulations dealing with the stability of priests in their parish assignments, trusteeism, the use of the Douay Bible (a seventeenth-century translation) as a standard text and the need for a uniform catechism as well as a Catholic school system. A clear sign of the times at the Second Provincial Council of 1833 was its concern with rising anti-Catholicism in the nation as new immigrants began to reach the American shore.

For Discussion

How does the "pioneer spirit" of independence enhance the American character? How does it affect community ties (religious or civil) and assistance to people in need?

In many ways, the most startling portion of the story of American Catholicism in the early nineteenth century was to occur on the western frontier. For Americans, the "West" had long been a state of mind as well as a geographical locale. It represented the constant appeal of new beginnings and seemingly endless opportunities. It suggested the need for a pioneer spirit undaunted by isolation, hardship, hard work and privation. Pioneers learned to live with an environment that was rural, a character that was independent and political realities that demanded innovation and experimentation.

To speak of Catholicism in the nineteenth century was to invoke images of a Church that was largely urban, traditional and authoritarian: the mirror opposite of all that the frontier represented. The prospects for Catholicism in the area looked dim indeed. And yet, by an amazing chemistry, Catholicism took to the frontier. Along with other believers who flocked to the area—Baptists, Methodists and Presbyterians—Catholics helped to bring stability, education and a sense of tradition to the great untamed region. In turn, these early Catholics would learn lasting lessons in religious pluralism and adaptability.

According to Alistair Cooke's study *America*, Kentucky was the "first American West." Admitted to the Union in 1792 as the fifteenth state, the first beyond the mountains, its star would be the first western one in the national flag. The flow of settlers to Kentucky was enormous; its population doubled to two hundred thousand by 1800. These stalwart pioneers, like their earlier forebears in the East, were not overly eager to join the established Churches. By no means a godless folk, they managed to combine their biblical piety with a stubborn individualism.

The "Second Great Awakening" of American religious history began among these people in 1801. The famous Cane Ridge Revival of that year saw up to twenty thousand individuals flocking to remote areas in order to subject themselves to intensive, highly emotional preaching by Protestant ministers. Thus did the southern revival tradition arise. Many of the congregation at Cane Ridge responded with such extraordinary behavior as fainting spells, the "jerks," chasing the devil or fits of uncontrolled laughter. The revival tripled memberships in many pioneer Baptist Churches and led to the eventual formation of the Disciples of Christ, a congregational, Scripture-based sect, as well as to the introduction of the celibate Shakers to Kentucky. Regional Catholics, publicly silent, reacted in private with scorn to such outbursts of religious emotion as "dying follies" and redoubled their efforts to spread the gospel through institutional means.

Across the frontier, in Catholic as well as Protestant churches, congregations often separated males from females. According to Kentucky historian James Robertson, Jr., one Protestant minister bemoaned the lack of frontier refinement as he tried to preach to an open-air assembly he described as "forty-five babies, seventy-five dogs, with only sixty adults to police the mob." In the more settled churches, Sunday sermons were generally ninety minutes long. While pioneer Catholics confided their sins in the confessional, many Protestant churches held a public accounting of misconduct. Thus can contemporary historians rank the main reasons for frontier moral correction: drunkenness, dancing, fornication, failure to attend church, adultery and swearing.

The diocese centered at Bardstown, a lively town in central Kentucky's Nelson County, was established in 1808 during this era of religious enthusiasm. It was initially vast, comprising the land from the Great Lakes to the deep South and from the Appalachian-Allegheny mountain chain to the Mississippi. Nearly thirty-six dioceses were later carved from this jurisdiction. Its first bishop was, like so many of the clerics in the years after 1790, an exile from the French Revolution.

A Bishop's Diary—1812

January 1 After hearing confessions all morning, I celebrated Mass at Holy Cross until 3:00 p.m.

January 2 I went to St. Charles. Confessions, Mass, sermons until 2:00 p.m.

January 6 Discontented, sad, troubled.

January 8 Visited a sick drunkard. I made him ask pardon publicly.

January 10 Assembled the people of St. Charles to discuss the priest's establishment. Great difficulties to overcome.

January 16 At Loretto, preached. Confessions until noon. Few persons. Feeble hope of success in affairs of the Church. Great confidence in God.

January 18 At the seminary. Correspondence. Theology. The seminarians seem more poised and happy. May it be given me to see them as fervent as angels.

January 20 Left for St. Stephen. Mr. Badin informed me of the news of the defeat of [Napoleon] Bonaparte.

January 26 Mr. Hirt's negress died without the sacraments. Could be my fault. Pardon me, Lord. My heart is broken with doubts.

January 30 The day is full as to time, but has the work been well done? Vanity, impatience, carelessness—have these not carried off the greater part of my merit? I tremble that even my good deeds will turn to my confusion. (From Benedict Joseph Flaget's 1812 diary.)

Bishop Benedict Joseph Flaget was the first bishop of Bardstown, Kentucky, a massive see from which some thirty-six dioceses were later carved.

(France's loss of so many priests in the Revolution worked decidedly to American Catholicism's gain.) Sulpician Benedict Joseph Flaget (1763-1850) would spend two years seeking to avoid his appointment to such a vast territory and task before he was finally consecrated by Bishop Carroll in 1810.

When the courtly, saintly Flaget arrived in Kentucky the following year to initiate the first inland diocese of the country, he oversaw an extraordinary outburst of Catholic energies that would eventually shape much of the early Church in the Midwest and upper South. Soon the Catholic culture within a forty-mile radius of tiny Bardstown was to rival Baltimore in institutional growth.

But the issue of lay leadership was vital on the frontier, too. Flaget found himself preaching to rural congregations about what he considered the excesses of trusteeism.

Even before the bishop's arrival, the Catholics of central Kentucky, transplanted Marylanders for the most part, had industriously built up a network of congregations. This western center of Catholicism was begun by leagues of laity who came out purposely to Kentucky in large groups beginning in 1785, so that they could eventually lay claim on Bishop Carroll for a cleric.

Sustaining their faith by familial solidarity and prayer manuals, they managed at best to attract clerics for brief periods of time until Father Stephen Badin's arrival in 1793 brought stability. But Badin's sometimes strict spirituality often resulted in harsh confessional penances, public acts of repentance and strictures against such frontier festivities as dances. The laity of the region were often outspoken in their opposition to Badin, most notably Grace Newton Simpson, recognized by her contemporaries as one of the keener theological minds in the wilderness. In 1805, the Dominican priests made their first foundation in the United States at Springfield, Kentucky, close by Bardstown.

The first decade of Flaget's forty-year term as bishop saw the opening of the first seminary and cathedral in the West; the growth of three colleges and the establishment of three native sisterhoods. The Sisters of Loretto began in April, 1812, when Mary Rhodes and two other local women received a rule from Belgian missionary Charles Nerinckx; theirs was to be the first American congregation not directly linked to a European motherhouse. That same December, the Sisters of Charity of

Nazareth were gathered together by John Baptist David, the rector of St. Thomas Seminary. In 1822 more Kentucky women, led by Angela Sansbury, united to form the first Dominican convent in America.

Soon these brimming communities and institutions were producing leaders not only for Kentucky, but for the Church across the nation. No less than eight of Flaget's priests would become bishops, including Francis Patrick Kenrick (1796-1863), later Bishop of Philadelphia; and Martin John Spalding (1810-1872), later Archbishop of Baltimore. The latter's cousin, the zealous Catherine Spalding (1793-1858), long led the Sisters of Charity of Nazareth, and was responsible in Louisville alone for the establishment of an academy, a hospital and an orphanage. Before the Civil War, hundreds of the sisters from Nazareth, Loretto and Springfield were active in service across the country. Shortly before his death, Flaget welcomed into his diocese the French Trappist monks who founded Gethsemani, the monastery that became internationally known in the twentieth century as the home of Thomas Merton.

The expansion of Catholics on the frontier was constant in those antebellum years. By 1836, Flaget estimated his flock at thirty-six thousand, larger than the Church in the entire country under Bishop Carroll in 1790. The subdivision of the Bardstown jurisdiction into new dioceses reveals dramatic growth: Cincinnati (1821); Vincennes, Indiana (1834); Nashville (1837); Detroit (1837); and Chicago (1843).

It was the nature of the American West in those years to be constantly moving *farther* west. This was especially true after President Thomas Jefferson's 1803 purchase from France of the vast Louisiana Territory. All or portions of fifteen states were later carved from this acquisition, which at a stroke doubled the size of the nation. St. Louis, the gateway to the new national heartland, hosted the next generation of fresh growth. That Midwestern metropolis had originally been part of the Diocese of Louisiana, based in New Orleans. But because of agitations in that city connected with the machinations of Père Antoine and the issue of trusteeism yet again, Bishop William DuBourg (1766-1833) chose to spend most of his time at St. Louis, where he was aided by Vincentian priests.

During DuBourg's term of office, Rose Phillippine Duchesne (1769-1852) arrived in the city with the first American foundation of her order, the Society of the Sacred

Mother Catherine Spalding cofounded the Sisters of Charity of Nazareth (Kentucky), which served students, orphans and the sick throughout the South and East, and eventually overseas as well.

_Enroute to Santa Fe, Sisters of
Loretto and Sisters of Charity
pause to bury Sister Mary
Alphonse Thompson, S.L., on
the plains._

Heart. Although she was active in educational ventures for
nearly thirty years, in retirement she went to live among the
Potawatomi Indians, who called her "the woman who always
prays." Pope John Paul II canonized the French-born Duchesne
in 1988.

DuBourg was also instrumental in the 1818 opening of the
academy that would evolve into St. Louis University. His
auxiliary bishop, Joseph Rosati (1789-1843), became bishop of
the new see of St. Louis, established in 1826.

For Discussion

Women religious were actively involved in the westward movement, staffing schools, hospitals and missions. Discuss the influence of these women on American Catholic life.

Although the missionaries in the Midwest ministered mainly to settlers of European stock, the missions to Native Americans were not neglected. A Jesuit based in St. Louis, Pierre de Smet (1801-1873), visited Indians in the Rocky Mountains, Montana and Oregon. Similarly, Frederic Baraga (1797-1868) turned his attention to tribes in Michigan, where Gabriel Richard (1767-1832) had preceded him. (Richard also helped found the University of Michigan and became the first priest to serve in the U.S. Congress.) Another missioner among Indians of the northern region in the 1830's was Dominican Samuel Mazzuchelli (1806-1864). Like Rose Phillippine Duchesne, hundreds of American sisters went to missions in the Southwest and Far West despite incredible hazards and hardships.

By the 1840's, Americans were beginning to pronounce themselves possessed of a "manifest destiny" to spread across the continent "from sea to shining sea." Largely due to their success in the Mexican War (1846-1848), they were able to realize such a dream. Catholicism in the early United States had, like the new nation itself, long clung to the eastern seaboard. For the first generation of national life, it had been a Church whose population lived primarily below the Mason-Dixon line. Within half a century of independence, both nation and Church expanded across a continent. As the 1840's dawned, the nation was poised to receive the greatest immigration of people in all recorded history. Neither nation nor Church would ever be quite the same again.

Part Three

The Immigration Era: From Manifest Destiny to the Gilded Age

Chapter Seven

An Immigrant Church

In the hundred years from the 1820's to the 1920's, before immigration to the United States was severely curtailed by Congress, over thirty million immigrants flowed into the expanding nation. The earliest wave came before the Civil War, primarily from Ireland and Germany. The postbellum throng traced their roots to eastern and southern Europe. The growing country badly needed raw energy and willing labor, and was pleased to accept the newcomers who were, for the most part, fleeing poverty or political turmoil in their homelands, and were lured to America by its promises of economic opportunity, security and freedom.

Though population numbers can often be dull, they tell a dramatic story of the effect of immigration on the size of the Catholic community. In 1820, one hundred ninety-five thousand Catholics lived in America; thirty years later, there were more than a million and a half. Within the decade from 1850 to 1860 alone, the Catholic population doubled to over three million. By 1920, it stood at eighteen million. Early in the twentieth century, the faithful were served by some eleven thousand priests and forty thousand sisters. The sisters of this era, judges historian James Kenneally in *American Catholic Women*, were "the force holding the Church together," for they "exercised the major influence on the growing immigrant population, and bore the economic brunt of selfless service."

Irish and German Catholics both crowded into the cities. The Irish tended to concentrate more in the East, while those of Teutonic blood flowed into the "German triangle" extending from Milwaukee to St. Louis to Cincinnati. In the Ohio city, the Germans built eleven parishes between 1835 and 1860, most notably in the "Over the Rhine" district, where they developed a culture distinctive in language and customs. For European immigrants generally and for the Germans in particular,

Would-be immigrants at Ellis Island, New York, which opened in 1892.

Anti-Catholic Editorials

A re men fit to be American voters, and especially are men fit to hold office...who regard themselves as owing to our government no allegiance from which the Pope of Rome, an inflated Italian despot who keeps people kissing his toes all day, cannot at any moment release them?

One [Know-Nothing Party] is a band of enlightened, educated, liberal, patriotic, native citizens; the other [party] is a combination of every faction, ism and sect from the foreign pest-houses and prisons to the rich and grasping Priests, Bishops and Archbishops.... Remember that your defeat may cause Rome to howl with the shouts of triumph of...the Hierarchy over the Republic.

Until the light of Protestantism shone in the world there was no religious freedom. Popery, with its iron heel, treads out the life of religious liberty as fast as it is born.... Rally to put down an organization of Jesuit bishops, Priests, and other papists, who aim by secret oaths and horrible perjuries and other midnight plottings, to destroy the foundation of all our political edifices. (George Prentice, *Louisville Journal*, August 1855)

For Discussion

Catholic immigrants were often unwelcome and met discrimination. Compare their situation with that of immigrant groups today.

maintaining their native language was a paramount concern. It was also a battleground within Catholicism with those eager to encourage full assimilation into American life.

With the rise of the Catholic population emerged also a virulent recurrence of anti-Catholicism. Many "nativists" clung to an image of the Church as a hierarchical, undemocratic institution that worshiped in a foreign tongue (Latin) and accepted political dictation from a foreign power (Rome). In addition, many of the newcomers were poor and were perceived as an economic threat who either drained the coffers of public charity or took jobs away from homegrown Americans. (American resistance to foreigners extends from the Irish and

Editor Orestes Brownson, Bishop Martin John Spalding and Paulist founder Father Isaac Hecker stressed the Catholic contribution to American life.

Germans in the nineteenth century down to Asians, Hispanics and Haitians in the late twentieth century.)

Understandably defensive, Catholic leaders emphasized the patriotism of their coreligionists during the nation's wars and insisted that the papacy wielded only spiritual influence over its faithful, never touching on matters temporal or political.

The nativist frenzy of paranoia persisted. Rumors threatened a papal takeover of the nation, starting, perhaps, with the Mississippi Valley. Samuel F. B. Morse (of telegraph fame) produced an 1835 book whose very title pronounced its theme: *The Foreign Conspiracy Against the Liberties of the United States.* The next year Maria Monk's potboiler *Awful Disclosures of the Hotel Dieu Nunnery of Montreal* appeared, purporting to tell of her unwilling entrapment in a Canadian convent. It contained lurid tales of priest-sister liaisons and of illegitimate infants buried in convent crypts.

Fear began to take visible and violent forms. In 1834, a convent and orphanage in the Charlestown area of Boston were burned to the ground by mob action. In 1844 Catholics in Philadelphia were assaulted by riots, while "Bloody Monday" mobs at Louisville in 1855 caused over twenty deaths. In California, nativism took on an anti-Hispanic hue. For a brief span in the 1850's the Know-Nothing political party came into prominence, fanning the fires of fear and prejudice. But all was not bleak; even in the midst of the fray, some Protestant ministers came forward in defense of their Catholic neighbors.

The new climate of fear and intimidation set the stage for a

Progress and Problems

And first, permit us to congratulate you on the progress that has been made by the aid of the Most High.... The number of our clergy has...considerably increased.... Our seminaries are enlarged.... The religious houses, especially of females, have been multiplied. There are retreats wherein justly many indulge their desire of frequent attendance upon the Lord, [and] in which the youthful mind is trained to industry, to science and to virtue.... Piety has diffused its influence widely through our flocks....

We must, however, deplore not only the guilt of the fabricators [of libels on Catholic character], but amongst the consequences of their misconduct, one to which it is not impossible to apply a remedy: the contamination of the minds of the delicate and the young, in these numerous families into which an unchecked spirit of bad curiosity..., of reckless hatred of our religion has introduced the polluting romances [novels].... Of the mass of these inventions which have been so extensively scattered abroad, several copies must descend to future generations.... (U.S. Catholic Bishops' Pastoral Letter, 1840)

new, more vigorous defense among leaders of Catholic thought. Such writers as Bishop Martin John Spalding (1810-1872), convert and founder of the Paulists Father Isaac Hecker (1819-1888) and lay leader and prolific editor Orestes Brownson (1803-1876) developed aggressively positive estimates of Catholics' contribution to American life.

For Spalding, the Catholic tradition (despite past excesses) had been the greatest force in Western history for human rights and dignity, and had ultimately made the modern expression of such rights possible. Beyond this historical argument, Spalding maintained that only the Catholic tradition, with its emphasis on balance, community and natural law, could keep America true to its destiny. Protestantism, for Spalding, only led the nation toward exaggerated individualism.

Hecker did not stress the past role of the Catholic

institution. Rather, he probed the deeply subjective and personal needs of the American people. These could best be served, Hecker was convinced, by the objective revelation of the Church and by a renewed Catholic awareness of the Holy Spirit's power, moving individuals and the nation toward greater freedom and accomplishment.

Brownson, who is buried at the University of Notre Dame, was a convert to Catholicism earlier associated with the Transcendentalist movement. As editor of *Brownson's Quarterly Review*, he consistently urged Catholics to become fully part of American life and culture—but he just as steadily urged the conversion of all America to Catholicism. He was uncomfortable with attempts to relate the theory of evolution to Church teaching. Brownson was not generally easy to classify as conservative or liberal, although his political and theological positions did tend to move to the right in later years.

While such thinkers sought to reclaim liberty as a predominantly Catholic theme, others, conservatively attuned, began to conceive of a more hierarchically structured Church whose great task was the *protection* of the Catholic people in a frequently hostile environment. Most outspoken of this wing of opinion was New York's fiery Archbishop John Hughes (1797-1864). Fearing the growing power of radical individualism and distrusting the growing emphasis on innate human nobility and goodness, he argued instead that humanity could rise above its sinfulness only by turning to the God of Revelation. That God, Hughes maintained, could be found fully only in the long tradition of Catholicism. Thus did he place himself squarely in opposition to the more optimistic views of such contemporaries as essayist Ralph Waldo Emerson and poet Walt Whitman.

Hughes himself found greater authority rather than greater liberty the key to a more virtuous life, whether private or civic. He is reputed to have uttered the dictum that he would suffer no man in his diocese that he could not control. When anti-immigrant violence threatened New York City parishes, he armed pastors with muskets for the defense of their properties. This stood in marked contrast to Bishop Spalding's handling of the crisis in Louisville: In the *Louisville Journal* he urged Catholics to pacific behavior in a time of "civic feuds and bloody strife."

Hughes was one of the many bishops who became

embroiled in the Church/State "textbook controversy." He argued that Catholic pupils in the public schools should not be forced to listen to Protestant versions of the Bible in moral instruction and prayer. The dispute not only accelerated the movement toward an alternative Catholic school system but also hastened the secularization of the public educational system.

Hughes's attitude in both theology and politics had considerable influence on subsequent American Catholicism. Hughes was joined in many of his new emphases by Philadelphia's sainted bishop, John Nepomucene Neumann (1811-1860) and even in some respects by Bishop Martin Spalding, Archbishop of Baltimore after 1864. (Neumann was a Redemptorist from Bohemia who caused eighty churches to be built in his diocese, increased the numbers of children in Catholic schools twenty-fold, and fostered the "Forty Hours" eucharistic devotion. In 1977 he was canonized, the first American bishop named a saint.) Such bishops were inclined not only to emphasize the distinctive roles of clergy and laity, but also to urge discipline, obedience to authority and constant self-scrutiny on their people. As a consequence, the faithful were expected to turn to the institutional Church as a place of spiritual refuge and moral protection.

Unlike the more British brand of spirituality in the Carroll era, when Catholic piety expressed itself in restrained personal devotion alongside the Mass and sacraments, the new immigrant spirituality emphasized human sinfulness and emotional, Church-based devotions. Processions, novenas, Forty Hours, pilgrimages and devotions to Jesus, Mary and the saints as fellow sufferers and protectors proliferated, especially in "national" or ethnic parishes. Such intensifications of piety and discipline were part of the growth of clerical authoritarianism in Rome. The popes of the mid-nineteenth century adopted such conservative attitudes (and encouraged them in America) in order to counter the rapid political and intellectual changes of the age, many of which had produced hostility to the Church.

Even the architecture of churches changed. Catholic houses of worship that once had copied the republican simplicity of their Protestant neighbors began to revel in ornate European styles of design and ornamentation. (Greater affluence was surely a factor; some Protestant churches were similarly

Bishop John Nepomucene Neumann of Philadelphia organized the first diocesan school system and encouraged Forty Hours devotion. He was canonized in 1977.

The interior of St. Augustine Church, Lebanon, Kentucky, which was built in 1871.

affected in post-Civil War America.) Churches became enclaves filled with statues and stained glass, evoking the majesty of the Catholic past and inviting parishioners into an otherwordly zone of solemnity and peace.

In the nation at large, this antebellum era was a time of continued westward expansion and restless moral energies. The ready acceptance of the writings of Congregationalist theologian Horace Bushnell (1802-1876) signalled the turn of American Protestant thought away from harsher Puritan beliefs and practices. Bushnell emphasized the redemptive possibilities locked inside nature and the human heart; the poetic rather than literal importance of doctrines; and a gentle,

Monks at work on the Gatehouse at Gethsemani Abbey in Kentucky at the beginning of the twentieth century.

nurturing approach to individuals in place of a scolding, restrictive one. In this same epoch, Emerson and the Transcendentalists had celebrated the nobility rooted in both nature and the human spirit. Influential Unitarian writers such as William Ellery Channing (1780-1842) and Theodore Parker (1810-1860) had suggested the near-perfectibility of the human condition through moral exertion. Even President Andrew Jackson in his 1829 inaugural address had proclaimed his belief that "man can become more and more endowed with divinity."

All this emphasis on perfectibility helped to fuel a widespread movement of utopians and reformers seeking the betterment (if not the perfection) of American life. Ideal societies were attempted: New Harmony, Indiana; Oneida, New York; Brook Farm in Massachusetts. Reformers turned their sights on what they considered the major moral evils of the age: slavery, urban poverty, alcoholism and the disenfranchisement of women. Dorothea Dix (1802-1887) turned her unrelenting attention to the frightful treatment meted out to the mentally ill across the country, while others labored for prison reform, hoping to turn the jails of the nation into true reformatories rather than places of cruelty and harsh retribution.

The institutional energies and priorities of antebellum American Catholicism, while sympathetic to many social ills, were directed more toward the immigrants whose needs it was called upon to serve at so many levels of life: poverty relief, employment search, health care, child care. Nevertheless, Catholicism manifested a special kinship to the driving passions of the age, particularly in two areas: monasticism and higher education.

Monasticism had emerged in the West in the early Middle Ages, taking shape from the Rule of St. Benedict. In medieval society, the monastery was not only a place where monks sought greater perfection under grace and the monastic rule; it was also a center of education and comprehensive care for the residents of the region. While America was undergoing its flirtation with ideal communities of all descriptions in the 1840's, Catholic monasticism, the oldest form of utopian community in the Western world, made its debut in the United States.

The Trappists had earlier attempted (unsuccessfully) to begin a monastery on the frontier at the start of the nineteenth century. The first monastic foundation to endure was begun at Latrobe, Pennsylvania, by Benedictine Boniface Wimmer in 1846. Six years later, Mother Benedicta Riepp initiated the first foundation of American Benedictine Sisters at St. Mary's, also in Pennsylvania. These Cassinese Benedictines were soon joined by monks of the Swiss-American congregation, who settled at St. Meinrad in southern Indiana in 1854.

Dozens of daughter-houses, priories and abbeys from these three foundations spread across the country within generations. Meanwhile, the French Trappist (Cistercian) monks who had established Gethsemani Abbey in Kentucky in 1848 also spread monasteries across the American landscape. Some monasteries, such as Indiana's Benedictine St. Meinrad, established seminaries; many others provided retreat facilities for the lay population.

The second area in which the best of the Christian Middle Ages reappeared in the New World Republic was the university. Such schools arose in medieval times as elaborations of cathedral schools. The Catholic concern for education had produced colleges early in the Republic's life, as we saw in Chapter Four. But with the 1840's, a new burst of intensity resulted in such establishments as Fordham in New York (1841), Notre Dame in Indiana (1842), Holy Cross in Worcester, Massachusetts (1843), Loyola in Baltimore (1852) and the University of San Francisco in 1855. By the century's end, there were some sixty Catholic colleges in the United States, including two of the first to be founded for the education of women: Notre Dame of Maryland, which became

The new University of Notre Dame in South Bend, Indiana, founded in 1842.

a four-year college in 1895, and Trinity College in Washington, opened in 1900.

Antebellum Catholics claimed one other part of their medieval legacy: cathedral-building. In the forty years after the first division of the Baltimore See, the number of American dioceses grew from five to fifty; each new center of the faith was called upon to provide a worthy cathedral church. In the 1840's, Cincinnati erected the stately St. Peter in Chains; New Orleans was constructing its famous St. Louis Cathedral on Jackson Square; Louisville was building the Cathedral of the Assumption, with one of the highest spires in America. In 1858, Archbishop Hughes of New York placed the cornerstone of St. Patrick's Cathedral, a Gothic wonder that is one of the largest churches in the Christian world.

With the exception of Roger Brooke Taney (1777-1864), the Supreme Court Chief Justice who upheld the rights of slave-owners in the infamous Dred Scott decision of 1857, few Catholics attained high political power in these antebellum years. In the port cities of the East, however, with the constantly growing political power of the immigrants, the stage was being set for urban political machines, often controlled by Catholic (particularly Irish) politicians, in the later part of the century. Catholics, too, could be insular, clannish and set in their ways.

As the Civil War drew closer, Catholics in America had become the largest religious tradition in the country. Urban, working-class and foreign-born, they had dramatically changed the texture of American life once so English and homogeneous. In the shelter of the Church, the immigrants found not only nurture and care, but a strong sense of identity as well.

With the terrible fratricidal war approaching, Catholics, like so many of their neighbors, still puzzled over the one great issue that was to sear the conscience and rip apart the nation, the worm in the apple of American perfectibility: slavery.

St. Peter in Chains Cathedral, renovated in the 1950's, still serves the Archdiocese of Cincinnati.

Chapter Eight

Civil War and Intellectual Challenge

The cathedral in Charleston, South Carolina, left in ruins by Civil War shelling.

The issue of slavery tore apart not only the United States but its religious allegiances as well. By the mid-1840's, the burning moral question had split the Presbyterian, Methodist and Baptist Churches into northern and southern jurisdictions. Throughout the antebellum years, the zealous voices of Christians could be heard on both sides of the question. Abolitionists claimed that enslavement of fellow human beings violated divine justice; proslavers insisted that slavery not only had biblical warrant, but also represented the most benevolent system of protection and economic security for black people.

As with most of the major religious groups of the country, abolitionism never gained a great hearing among the American Catholic population. In fact, the three best-known Catholics of the early nineteenth century—Archbishop John Carroll, Declaration of Independence signer Charles Carroll and Chief Justice Roger Taney—had all been slaveholders, as had many religious communities, both male and female. True, Pope Gregory XVI in the late 1830's condemned the slave trade, but American supporters of the institution could claim that his holiness had not addressed the question of America's own domestic arrangement.

The premier Catholic moral theologian of his day, Francis Patrick Kenrick, had argued that slaves should not be mistreated and should have the right to marry and maintain their families; but that, for the sake of good order, priests should urge slaves to accept their lot. Not only did the Catholic newspapers in such southern climes as Charleston and Louisville oppose abolition, but those in Boston and New York did the same. Meanwhile Catholic publishers in the teeming city of Cincinnati and in the quiet village of Los Angeles

For Discussion

How do you account for Catholic insensitivity to the slavery issue and to the needs of ex-slaves? How do you rate Catholic concern for race relations today? Give your reasons.

85

expressed unrelenting opposition to slavery.

Two guiding ideals of the American Republic had long been enshrined in the evocative words *liberty* and *union*. These had appeared in campaign slogans and banners, and had been invoked as sacred syllables by orators and statesmen. But could these two eminently desirable realities dwell together in fact in so diverse and far-flung a nation? The Civil War was not only to test a nation and its people; it was to be a metaphysical battleground as well, as the forces of individual liberty (states' rights) and corporate solidarity (the Union) struggled in deadly combat.

Presiding over the Union cause was Abraham Lincoln, a complex leader judged by some historians the most mystical of the presidents. Lincoln clearly knew and revered the Bible, but committed himself to no particular denomination. While the sixteenth president did not believe in full equality of the races, he stood in sympathy with the abolitionists.

As the war advanced, Lincoln found it personally desirable and tactically advantageous to offer the nation a higher moral purpose for the hostilities by issuing the Emancipation Proclamation. Yet even this was enacted to achieve a purpose that Lincoln considered higher still: the preservation of the Union. That very word assumed for Lincoln a near-mystical quality. He called his country "the last, best hope of Earth," and was convinced that should the union of the states be sundered, all the Enlightenment principles for which America stood in the eyes of the nations would be shattered as well.

The more zealous Catholic advocates of the era were quick to lay the ultimate blame for any divisiveness in the United States not so much in the political as in the theological realm. At New York's Catholic *Freeman's Journal*, the highly controversial and reactionary editor James McMaster ran an explosive series of articles in the summer of 1861. On June 22 the *Journal* assured its readers: "If the [United States] perishes now..., it will be for lack of the Catholic religion." An unsigned diatribe in the edition of August 3 (probably from McMaster's own pen) noted the divisions that had taken place in so many Protestant denominations, only to remark that Protestantism "is full of schisms and goes on rending and being rent." In the process, the writer insisted, the "Protestant sects...in working the ruin of the country...have exposed...the hollowness of Protestantism and its destructive and separating tendencies.

For Discussion

What truth or falsity do you see in the proposition that Catholicism unites; Protestantism divides?

James McMaster, reactionary editor of New York's Catholic Freeman's Journal, *attacked Protestantism as a divisive force.*

They have destroyed the old Constitution of the country."

In short, the *Journal* was saying that Protestantism divides; Catholicism unites, that a theological civil war had been raging in America for decades before military hostilities began. After the Emancipation Proclamation was enacted in January 1863, Louisville Bishop Martin John Spalding confided to the privacy of his diary that Lincoln's signing of the document showed that "Puritanism with its preachers and Common Schools has at last ruined the country." Such antiecumenical sentiments were rarely so blatantly expressed in Catholic circles, but their occasional appearance indicated that the war was being interpreted among some Catholics in nearly cosmic terms.

The vast majority of American Catholics, both lay and clerical, did not trouble themselves with such metaphysical concerns, but plunged instead into the practical necessities of wartime. Catholics donned the blue or the gray, largely on the basis of their geographical location. In Charleston, Bishop Patrick Lynch ordered a *Te Deum* sung in celebration at his cathedral after the fall of Fort Sumter; in the New York cathedral, Archbishop Hughes hung the Stars and Stripes and urged his faithful to serve the Union. At Richmond, Bishop John McGill blessed the infantry pikes of Confederate troops in the crypt of his cathedral; in Louisville a pastor scolded an organist for weaving "Dixie" into the recessional at Mass.

At Baltimore's cathedral, Archbishop Kenrick ordered the recitation of Bishop Carroll's prayer for the government (see p. 51) at all Masses, only to find southern sympathizers rustling papers loudly in protest. In Confederate Nashville, the decidedly pro-Union Bishop James Whelan resigned his post in the middle of the war.

During the summer of 1863, after Lincoln had ordered the first national draft with a provision exempting those who could pay three hundred dollars, rioting broke out in New York City, particularly among poor Irish, who were most susceptible to induction. After the Emancipation Proclamation, one of the war's explicit aims became the freeing of slaves. The impoverished and draft-prone now found themselves compelled to do battle against slavery itself. Consequently, the fracases that ensued often pitted Irish immigrants against free black scapegoats in New York. The violence in that city rivaled the Los Angeles riot of 1992—seventy-four deaths and

Sisters of Mercy as Nurses in the Civil War

A t the close of the second day's struggle at Shiloh, ten thousand soldiers lay lifeless upon the battlefield.... On the steamer...the dangerously wounded were placed in a secluded section. Here was a flag-bearer whose arm was badly shattered, his neighbor had been shot through the lungs.... Another cot was occupied by an officer whose two mutilated legs had been amputated.... In the midst of this tragedy Mother Theresa Maher was always calm and efficient. To each soldier, sick or wounded, she tried to distribute an equal share of attention....

[The ship went to Cincinnati and the wounded were transferred to a hospital.] In the midst of these heart-breaking scenes, which seemed the acme of human suffering, "smallpox in the hospital" was announced in whispers, and then, as the dread disease advanced, many attendants fled in dismay. The Sisters, however, remained during this awful calamity.... With her own hands, Mother Theresa Maher dressed the wounds of the afflicted.... There were other Sisters of Mercy of her community who, actuated by divine love and pity, stood day and night by the cots of the men writhing in the agonies of a gruesome affliction. (From *Nuns of the Battlefield*, by Ellen Jolly)

widespread property damage—and troops had to be called in from the field of Gettysburg to restore order.

Throughout the conflict, over five hundred sisters from a score of communities performed the difficult service of battlefield nurses for both sides. Forty priests were in military service as chaplains for the Stars and Stripes; another thirty for the Confederate Banner. In the South, Catholic churches and institutions were often pressed into service as hospitals. Occasionally they were completely destroyed, as was the cathedral at Charleston. Catholic newspapers, academies and colleges were forced to suspend their operation due to economic and transportation problems.

Sister Anthony O'Connell, S.C., was depicted in a 1915 oil painting by Ernestine Fashey, S.C., as the "Angel of the Battlefield" during the Civil War.

Two bishops in particular fought the war out verbally (though ever so politely) along the borderland of the Ohio River, the old barrier between free and slave territory. At Cincinnati (where Harriet Beecher Stowe, author of *Uncle Tom's Cabin*, had resided), Archbishop John Purcell had urged emancipation months before Lincoln acted. His newspaper, the *Catholic Telegraph*, maintained an abolitionist position. Just downriver at Louisville, Bishop Martin John Spalding presided over a diocese that included over two thousand Catholic slaves and whose journal, *The Guardian*, argued loudly against abolition. Spalding reported Purcell to Rome as being among the "party of blood," and in 1863 wrote a special analysis of the war for the Vatican, which found its way into the official Roman paper, *Osservatore Romano*.

Spalding, who was elevated in 1864 to the post of Archbishop of Baltimore, struck a restrained and judicious note in his report. Whereas the solution chosen by the South—secession—could indeed lead to anarchy, he allowed, that of the North could result in tyranny. The hostilities had resulted, he insisted, not just because of the slavery issue, but also because of a tariff which enriched the industrial North at the expense of the agricultural South. Gradual emancipation alone could save the situation, Spalding maintained, and that could take place only if a steady Catholic influence prevailed in American affairs.

Although he did not make it part of his official report, the southern bishop was personally convinced that the war would end with an independent Confederacy intact. According to historian James Kenneally, Pope Pius IX may have been of the same opinion. The pontificate of that conservative, the longest in history (1846-1878), was complicated by the struggle of Italian nationalists to unify the nation—a process blocked by the continued existence of the Papal States across the geographical center of the Italian peninsula. In 1870, the unification forces seized the papal properties, and modern-day Italy came into existence.

The United States had not been at all supportive of the pontiff in his conflict with the forces pushing for a unified Italy. Perhaps fearing a victorious Union as too strong a force in world affairs, the pope, said British diplomat Odo Russell in the summer of 1864, "would not conceal from me the fact that all his sympathies were with the Southern Confederacy."

The first postwar gathering of the Catholic bishops of the United States took place at the Second Plenary Council of Baltimore in 1866. At its conclusion, the prelates issued a lengthy pastoral letter to the American faithful, touching on such varied topics as the sacredness of marriage, the danger of a rising divorce mentality in the land and the encouragement of the Catholic press as well as Catholic industrial schools in which "the youthful culprit may cease to do evil and learn to do good."

A special section of the pastoral urged special care and education for the newly freed blacks "with their peculiar dispositions and habits." Still, the bishops expressed their regret, noting that "a more gradual system of emancipation could have been adopted."

In the early 1870's, two missionary communities, the Mill Hill Fathers and the Congregation of the Holy Ghost, came from England to the United States to work among freed blacks. Even before the war, two communities of black sisters had been successfully established in the country: the Oblate Sisters of Providence at Baltimore in 1829, and the Sisters of the Holy Family at New Orleans in 1842. Both before and after the war, various communities of sisters (such as the Sisters of St. Joseph of Carondelet at St. Louis in 1845) attempted schools for black children, at times being forced to close down because of threats of violence. In his Savannah diocese, Bishop Augustin Verot, one of the most aggressively proslavery bishops before the Civil War, became one of the prelates most solicitous for the

Children of the "colored school" staffed by the Sisters of Loretto at Lebanon, Kentucky, in 1884.

Bishop James Augustus Healy of Portland, Maine, the son of a slave, was the first black American bishop.

pastoral care of the newly emancipated.

In 1875, James Augustine Healy (1830-1900), son of a slave mother, was named bishop of Portland, Maine. His brother Patrick, a Jesuit, served as president of Georgetown University from 1874-1882. Although they were the first black Catholics in the nation to serve as a bishop and a college president, neither became known as a spokesman for or strong supporter of his race. A modern-day black Catholic historian, Cyprian Davis, cautions in *The History of Black Catholics in the United States* against too harsh a judgment on the Healy brothers by latter-day standards, yet wonders "how these good and upright men judged themselves in the silence of their own hearts."

The Conversion of America to the Catholic Faith

That our country is to be, and will be, converted to Catholicity is a proposition no Catholic will dare to controvert. The Catholic Church prays and labors for this conversion;...she labors for it with unwearied energy....

Political persecution and social ostracism are doing their work. The Catholics in this country have been surrounded by an overwhelming, bigoted, proscriptive, persecuting Protestant majority. As a rule, the avenues of wealth, honors, social position and political ambition have been closed to the Catholic. The influences of education, fashion and worldliness have combined to separate the American Catholic from the religion of his ancestors.

The first thing to be done...as a work of preparation for the conversion of America is a practical showing forth of the true influence of Catholicity in the lives of its professors [through temperance, cleanliness, frugality, education and intelligence]. If all the professed Catholics in the United States lived up to the requirements of their faith, their good example alone would be sufficient means for the conversion of America. (From the Baltimore *Catholic Mirror*, 1860)

All told, the Catholic stance was not impressive. In *American Catholicism*, the judicious historian Father John Tracy Ellis bluntly asks what the Church accomplished for the emancipated slaves. And he answers just as directly: "If one thinks in terms of the nearly four million Negroes involved, relatively little."

Most of the nearly fifty bishops present at the Second Plenary Council of Baltimore were also to take part in the First Vatican Council held at St. Peter's in Rome during 1869 and 1870. This first council since Trent (1545-1563) was the first major ecumenical council to witness American participation.

The Church in Europe was still reeling from the effects of such liberal ideas as freedom of speech and press unleashed by the French Revolution. Pope Pius IX had summarized what he categorized as the excessive liberties being taken in the modern age in his landmark *Syllabus of Errors* in 1864. The Council that gathered in 1869 was suffused with the fear of modernity and the sense that an authoritative center of truth had been lost. Not surprisingly, the key agenda item at Vatican I dealt with the reassertion of authority, most notably the definitions of papal primacy and infallibility.

Of the American bishops in attendance at the Council, some eighty percent initially did not favor the definition of papal infallibility, most on the basis that such a declaration would be "inopportune." These prelates came from a country that had seen more than its share of anti-Catholic agitation. They had for decades sought to reassure the American people that Catholics were patriotic citizens of undivided allegiance. Accordingly, their great fear was that a reassertion of papal power could set off new troubles at home.

In the end, however, the dogma of papal infallibility was solemnly proclaimed on July 18, 1870, during a ferocious Roman thunderstorm. Most Americans present came round to agreement with the modified definition of infallibility: papal power exercised only on solemn occasions and on faith and morals alone. Bishop Edward Fitzgerald of Little Rock was one of only two bishops in the world to vote no.

While the bishops struggled with such questions of doctrine at Rome, the American nation found itself in the midst of a tortured Reconstruction period, as well as facing the crises of industrialization, urbanization and unchecked immigration. America was entering in fact what Mark Twain was to describe as "the Gilded Age," an era that presented a bright external appearance but was nonetheless riddled with problems, corruption and contradictions.

And while America was shakily coming to terms with modernity and with a welter of new inventions (electric lighting and power, the telephone, the phonograph), an intellectual revolution was brewing as well. Beneath the placid surface that people today associate with Victorian America, the groundwork was being laid for startling challenges to traditional modes of thought.

Biblical studies in Germany (popularized in America in part through the work of French scholar Ernst Renan) radically questioned the literal understanding of basic Scripture texts. Closer to home, by century's end, William James and John Dewey developed a philosophy that came to be known as pragmatism, placing the ultimate truth not in an accurate internal perception of external reality, but in the practical and the workable. Dewey also urged experimentation and experience in educational methods rather than rote learning. Ideas, James wrote—as only an American could do—had "cash value." Tradition and authority were not to be valued as much as experimentation and innovation.

In England, Darwin's *Origin of Species* (1859) and *The Descent of Man* (1871) posited a new account of creation. The world, by this reading, had not come into existence full-formed six thousand years ago. Rather it had evolved over millions of years through "natural selection" and "survival of the fittest." Such an account could be readily reconciled with belief in a Creator God—provided one did not take Genesis literally as a "scientific" presentation.

But Darwin's challenge went beyond a mere threat to a fundamentalist reading of biblical creation. Such studies offered an alternate explanation of how the world came to assume its present configuration that need not exclude divinity, but did not insist upon it.

In the social order, Karl Marx (1818-1883) urged a revolutionary reconstruction of the social order, denying private property as well as the rights of religion, which he considered an obstacle to human progress. The German thinker had argued that the "have-nots" of the world (the proletariat) were being robbed of their time and labor by starvation wages paid them by the "haves" (capitalists). Only a revolution, Marx

For Discussion

Discuss the challenge presented to the American Churches by Marx, Darwin and Freud. Are they still a challenge to belief? Why or why not?

wrote, could put production into the hands of the workers. Forgetting completely the Jewish and Christian tradition of prophets and saints who cried out against social injustice, he argued that religion invariably supports the powerful against the powerless by turning attention away from the present crisis to the bliss of the hereafter. Much of the strong social justice teaching of the twentieth-century Church has come forth not only as a moral response to new social needs and crises, but also in response to the sort of criticism of faith offered by Marx and his followers.

By the century's end, Viennese psychologist Sigmund Freud (1856-1939) effected a psychological revolution that, like Marx's political one, denigrated religion, explaining human drives and motivations only in physical and psychological terms devoid of any ultimate spiritual significance. Darwin, Marx and Freud swept aside the traditional religious basis for asserting human destiny and establishing ideals for human behavior. In addition, they often presented the basic forces that drive human endeavor as outside of an individual's control—in biological urges, social forces or psychological complexes.

Many now grant that all three of these seminal thinkers, whose thought quickly crossed the Atlantic, produced ideas that, refined and modified, could stretch humanity's mind and its options. Marx, for example, pointed graphically to abuses and oppressions prevalent in nineteenth-century society; many of these same abuses were condemned as well by Pope Leo XIII in his *Rerum Novarum* (1891).

The stage had clearly been set for new, conflicting visions of humanity, and for a wrenching reevaluation of values. In the face of such unprecedented challenges, not Catholicism alone but all the traditional faiths of America found themselves in a crucible of change and complexity. As the United States celebrated the centenary of the Declaration of Independence in 1876 and passed into its second century of national life, many a new intellectual and spiritual mine field waited. And the Churches of America had before them a new agenda of staggering dimensions.

Chapter Nine

A Solid Catholic Culture

There were scattered signs across Catholic America in the Gilded Age that the new tide of ideas had won a hearing, though there was certainly not complete agreement. A small group of New York priests known as the Accademia raised questions on a range of issues from the value of a separate Catholic school system to clerical celibacy. One of their leaders, Edward McGlynn (1837-1900), was excommunicated for a time because of his highly vocal support of economist Henry George's single tax theory, which held that ultimately land and wealth belong to all—not only to the rich. He proposed a single tax on land to relieve the poor of tax burdens while drawing financial resources from those most able to pay.

In 1889 an idea long aborning, the Catholic University of America, opened in Washington. With the special drive of Bishop John Lancaster Spalding (1840-1916) and the substantial donation of convert Mary Gwendoline Caldwell (1863-1909), the university began with the goal of becoming something like a Catholic Harvard, providing Catholic leaders for America with a solid grounding in tradition as well as in the intricacies of modern thought.

Children from an Italian parish in Washington, D.C., on their First Communion day.

But the greatest expression of openness to the modern, especially the best of the American experience, was to come from a group of bishops who came to be known as the "Americanists." Most notably, these included John Ireland (1838-1918), archbishop of St. Paul; John J. Keane (1839-1918), rector of the Catholic University of America; and Denis J. O'Connell (1849-1927), rector of the North American College in Rome. Cardinal James Gibbons (1834-1921) of Baltimore and Bishop Spalding were frequent allies as well.

The Americanists generally accepted, perhaps at times uncritically, the nation's messianic sense of a mission to spread its liberties and system of government around the globe. Theirs

Archbishop John Ireland of St. Paul was one of the more notable "Americanists."

was an optimistic view of human nature, a belief that humanity was progressing steadily toward a richer future. The Churches—especially Catholicism with its heritage of community and critical intellect, had a key role to play in the humanizing of society. Thus were the old concept of manifest destiny and the new Catholic liberalism brought together in an unlikely marriage.

Not surprisingly, those who favored this liberal approach tended to be more supportive of the growing labor movement, of greater cooperation with other faiths and of a more thorough mainlining of Catholics, especially immigrants, into American society. They shared in some measure the perspective of Isaac Hecker that they lived in a new age of the Holy Spirit, in which private discernment and initiatives were to be encouraged.

None was more outspoken than Archbishop Ireland in his enthusiasm for American freedom, optimism and the activism of the new age. "I preach the new, the most glorious crusade," Ireland thundered. "Church and age! Unite them in the name of humanity, in the name of God." The America Republic he envisioned in nearly mystical terms: "For myself, I have unwavering faith in the Republic of America. I have faith in the providence of God and the progress of humanity."

The Church had much to learn from citizens' liberty and initiatives in the Republic, according to the Archbishop of St. Paul. Laypersons no longer need wait for direction from priests on social involvement, Ireland taught, nor priests wait on bishops. "The timid move in crowds; the brave in single file." He urged Catholics to rush "into the arena" to seek out social evils, and "lead in the movements that tend to rectify them."

Called the "Catholic Emerson" for his lucidity and elegance, the more aristocratic Spalding was not as comfortable with popular sovereignty as Ireland. Nevertheless, he argued strongly for the rights of women, lambasted those who sent children off to labor in factories and challenged a social system that made the few rich through the meagerly paid labor of many.

Ranged on the conservative side of this debate of the 1880's and 1890's were Jesuit theologians, several bishops—most notably Michael Corrigan (1839-1902) of New York and Bernard McQuaid (1823-1909) of Rochester—and many leaders of the German-American community, who especially rejected attempts at cultural and linguistic assimilation. The

'A National Calamity':
The Assassination of President McKinley (1901)

A s a people we are wanting in respect for those who are clothed with authority. We lack reverence; we are too ready to persuade ourselves that all is well so long as wealth and population increase. We seek facile solutions to great problems.

There is not now and never has been a civilized people. Ignorance, sin, depravity, injustice, cruelty, deceit, greed and selfishness have always prevailed and still prevail in the world. The majority has never loved nor does it now love truth and mercy and purity and holiness. But we more than any other people are dedicated to the securing of the largest freedom, the fullest opportunity, the completest justice to all, to men and women, to the strong and the weak, to the rich and the poor. (John Lancaster Spalding)

For Discussion

To what extent do immigrants still try to maintain their native language and customs? Do you think this is a good idea? Why or why not?

Germans, in fact, had a movement of their own led by Peter Cahensly (1838-1923) that argued for greater ethnic identity as the best way to keep Catholicism pure. Uncritical overidentification with American ways had already seriously compromised the faith, conservatives held. The Italian-American newspaper *The True American Catholic* overstated the case: "Christ himself is Roman."

From the perspective of a century later, historian David O'Brien judges in *Public Catholicism* that "conservatives, by overemphasizing the gap between Church and world, risked isolation from the age and irresponsibly disregarding its problems." But the liberals for their part, underestimated the "dangers posed by individualism, science and historical consciousness, [and] risked surrendering to the age." The liberals were also insufficiently self-critical and failed to value ethnicity.

The high water mark of the liberal bishops' activities was Catholic participation in the World Parliament of Religions at

The Role of the Catholic Woman in Society, 1893

The Catholic Women's Congress met in Chicago in May 1893 to consider the work of Catholic women. Out of the enthusiasm awakened by the Congress grew a National League to promote the spread of Catholic reading circles, temperance activities, day nurseries and kindergartens, protective and employment agencies for women, and social clubs and residences for young working women. Among the League's founders was Alice Timmons Toomey.

Mankind has repeated the "Our Father" for well-nigh two thousand years, and yet the great body of humanity seems only now waking up to the fact that "*our* Father" implies a common brotherhood; that "no man liveth to himself alone"; that we are our brother's keepers. Surely, then, in the face of these facts, it can only be through misapprehension of terms that the question is asked, "Is there a public sphere for Catholic women?" As well as ask, "Is there a public sphere for the religious?" since who is so public as the man or woman who gives his whole life, with all its powers, for the good of humanity? (Alice Toomey)

the 1893 Chicago World's Fair. There Cardinal Gibbons shared the stage not only with leaders of American Protestants and Jews, but also with Hindus, Buddhists and Muslims from around the world. But the tide was turning in a more conservative direction. In 1893, over the discreet objections of many bishops, who felt he might be perceived as a "Vatican spy," Archbishop Francesco Satolli arrived in Washington as the first apostolic delegate to the United States.

Acting very much as the eyes, ears and voice of the Vatican among the American bishops, Satolli was responsible for the development of a more cautious and conservative climate in American Catholic life. In 1895 Bishop O'Connell was relieved as rector of the North American University in Rome; Keane was removed as rector of Catholic University in 1896.

In 1899, Pope Leo XIII issued his famous letter *Testem*

Cardinal James Gibbons of Baltimore, whose liberalism troubled Rome, became one of organized labor's strongest supporters.

For Discussion

Pope Leo XIII was leery of such things as the separation of Church and State, activism and ecumenism. What reasons can you offer for his caution? Do you think these things are still under suspicion? Why or why not?

Benevolentiae, condemning the heresy he labeled "Americanism." The pope was careful to insist that he was not being negative about the American government or political system; but he *was* denying the enthusiastic insistence of those who saw the American separation of Church and State as an ideal for all the world. Additionally, the pontiff cautioned against excessive activism on the part of clergy or laity at the expense of the "passive" virtues, such as humility and obedience; and he discouraged experimentation in interfaith relationships.

Still fearful of rapid modern changes, the Vatican put a brake on creativity in favor of maintaining the traditional. Modern historians also note that the papal letter followed hard upon America's 1898 victory over Catholic Spain and may have been a subtle way of discouraging the victory of America's philosophies in reaction to its military triumph.

The Spanish-American War came at a time when the nation was in an imperialistic mood. As a result of the hostilities, the United States acquired Guam, the Philippines and Puerto Rico. In point of fact, most Catholics had been enthusiastic for their nation's role in the Spanish-American War. The irrepressible Bishop Denis O'Connell maintained that the battle pitted "all that is old and vile and mean and rotten..." in Europe against all that is "free and noble and open and true" in America.

Bishop Spalding was not so eager, cautioning his audiences about the dangers of imperialism. Editor Lawrence H. Bell of the *Catholic Advocate* similarly warned his coreligionists about a growing American tendency "to forget the plan and purpose of her government, a temptation to become one of the conquering, grasping powers of the world...."

Liberal American Catholic leaders were quick to give their assent to Pope Leo's letter, protesting all the while that the errors it defined were Europe-based and not really a significant part of the American scene. In 1907 Pope Pius X roundly condemned another movement—Modernism—that had arisen after 1890, principally in France, England and Italy. Modernism attempted to blend Catholic tradition more fully with emerging modern thought, especially in such areas as evolutionary biology, psychology, pragmatic philosophy and critical biblical scholarship.

The pope tended to see Modernism as a concerted movement. Even historians who appreciate some of the pope's fears have debated whether Modernism was truly an organized movement, and if the pope truly understood the Modernist writers in their full context. In any case, Pius X's repression of Modernism made original theological thinking suspect in Catholicism worldwide and in the United States for the next half a century.

In the area of labor and capital, however, a more liberal perspective prevailed. In the years after the Civil War, labor unions were established across the nation, often in the face of mighty opposition. The Knights of Labor, one of the earliest, was founded in 1869 and boasted a heavily Catholic immigrant membership. Union membership initially involved secret rituals and some of the early leaders were perceived by the bishops as leaning toward socialism. Bishop James Healy of Portland, Maine, excommunicated men in his diocese who belonged to the semisecret society. And in Canada the Knights were considered dangerous enough to be condemned by Catholic authorities.

At this time the leader of the American hierarchy, Cardinal James Gibbons of Baltimore, already revered for his book *The Faith of Our Fathers* (1876), made a dramatic intervention with the Roman authorities to prevented a similar condemnation in the United States.

While the Knights themselves were a short-lived phenomenon, American Catholic support for labor was firmly established. The initiative in the labor movement was clearly taken by lay Catholic leaders such as Terence Powderly (1849-1924), mayor of Scranton, Pennsylvania, in the 1880's. Some few clerics took up the cause before Gibbons emerged as one of organized labor's greatest protectors. "If the Church did not protect the working man," Gibbons later recalled, "she would have been false to her whole history."

The 1891 papal encyclical *Rerum Novarum* gave support to labor's rights to both unions and a living wage. The encouragement of both Gibbons and Pope Leo XIII would enable a much more visible Catholic labor movement to appear in the middle years of the twentieth century.

The most significant official gathering affecting Catholic life in the late nineteenth century was the Third Plenary Council of Baltimore in 1884. The seventy-two prelates in attendance reflected rapid Catholic growth across the country over the previous half century. Especially in the West, new

For Discussion

Is support for workers' rights still strong in Catholic circles? Why or why not?

dioceses had been established: Dubuque, Iowa (1837); Oregon City (1846); Santa Fe, New Mexico (1853); San Francisco (1853); Leavenworth, Kansas (1877); Helena, Montana (1884). Within three years of the Baltimore meeting, Omaha, Nebraska, and Denver were also made see cities.

The Council made the strongest call yet for schools in every parish; it also mandated a uniform teaching manual known to generations thereafter as the *Baltimore Catechism*. The bishops at Baltimore also insisted that the clergy wear cassocks in the rectory and the "Roman" collar in public. As old photographs attest, American priestly attire before this date often amounted to a dark suit with collar and tie. The imposition of *Roman* fashion was freighted with symbolism. The stateside Church was becoming more and more attuned to Roman centralization: in the creation of monsignors (honorary attendants at the papal throne); in sending the brightest clerical prospects to Rome for seminary education; in the increase of pious European devotions heavily indulgenced by the pope.

In 1884, the bishops of the United States gathered in Baltimore for the Third Plenary Council.

Meanwhile, a second wave of immigrants from southern and eastern Europe had begun to flow into the country. The Catholic community was growing at the staggering rate of nearly two million per decade. In the thirty years after 1880, the American Catholic population more than doubled to reach sixteen million, representing seventeen percent of the nation. From mid-century onward, the sisters teaching in the Catholic schools had been augmented by such male communities as the Xaverian Brothers and Christian Brothers. Largely thanks to the sisters, Catholicism by 1885 counted two hundred fifty orphanages, one hundred fifty hospitals and forty-five industrial schools across the nation.

The congregation of St. Charles Church in Marion County, Kentucky, in their Sunday finery.

In the half century after 1870, nearly four million Italians reached American shores, including St. Frances Xavier Cabrini (1850-1917), whose sisters worked in orphanages, schools and

St. Frances Xavier Cabrini and her sisters served the needs of the four million Italian immigrants who came to the United States in the half-century after the Civil War.

prisons across the continent. Two million Poles arrived in the same era, as well as one million French Canadians and a quarter-million Mexicans. From eastern Europe came some five hundred thousand Slovaks and over a quarter million each Lithuanians, Ukrainians and Czechs. And yet, so entrenched had Irish influence grown in the American Church that in 1900, over two-thirds of the bishops were of Irish extraction. (By 1870, the Irish were the largest ethnic group in the nation, representing nearly thirty-three percent of the total population.)

For the great majority of arriving Europeans, the parish was far more than a place of worship. It was one of the three institutions on which the newly arrived relied most heavily for socialization and survival. (The other two are said to be the political club and the saloon.)

With a new array of societies, sodalities and clubs, the parish often was the major cultural and social center in an ethnic neighborhood. Here human needs were served; here an immigrant's fragile sense of identity could be safeguarded and enhanced. And yet the best historical estimates suggest that less than half of those on the parish rolls attended church regularly in this era. (Laments about irregular church attendance, still voiced in our own time, are nothing new on the American Catholic scene.)

Many immigrants of the post-Civil War "second wave" settled in the rapidly growing steel center at Pittsburgh and in such industrial Great Lakes cities as Chicago, Detroit, Cleveland, Milwaukee, Erie and Buffalo. Many of the newcomers were Eastern-rite Catholics. Their Byzantine liturgies and spiritualities seemed exotic to many longer-established Catholics. Groups such as the Ruthenians (from the Austrian Empire) and the Ukrainians (from the Russian Empire) began to arrive by the late nineteenth century. By the early 1900's, Eastern-rite Catholics had come to the United States in such numbers that Rome granted them separate *eparchies* (dioceses). Some Latin-rite bishops tried to push these Catholics into Western liturgical observances, but Pope Pius XI in 1929 upheld their right to their own traditions—except a married clergy.

Many American Catholics today belong to four major Eastern traditions: Antiochene (Maronite Rite), Armenian, Chaldean and Constantinopolitan (the most extensive, including Melkite-Greek, Romanian, Ruthenian, Russian and

Gleanings From the *Baltimore Catechism*

Many editions of the Baltimore Catechism, derived from the Third Plenary Council at Baltimore in 1884, contained a "Do You Know?" section that was meant to enliven the study by putting cases before the class for consideration. Some examples:

Bertha, a non-Catholic, says: "I think it is awful that your Church gives indulgences to you Catholics so that you can commit a certain number of sins." What would you tell Bertha to correct her *wrong* idea of indulgences?

Marie, who was very sick, broke her fast before Holy Communion. Early each morning her mother gave her a large pill and a cup of thick gruel (a liquid form of oatmeal boiled in milk) before receiving. Why would you say this is correct?

Jacob died without becoming a Catholic. Walter, his Catholic friend, had warned him and had tried very hard to get him to study the Catholic religion. But Jacob would always say: "I'm too busy, and I have enough duties already." Why do you think that very likely Jacob is not saved?

Aloysius was always a good man and did whatever he thought God wanted him to do. But he died without becoming a Catholic. Why do you think that he very likely is saved?

Agnes sings well. Whenever anybody asks her to sing, she does her best. Afterwards when they say nice things about her singing, she thanks them and says: "Of course I know I am not the best singer in the world." Which moral virtue is Agnes practicing?

Why is it impossible for angels to have bodily wings of their own?

Why should you not entirely be afraid of the devil?

Ukrainian rites). Most of the Eastern rite churches, many topped by the traditional onion-dome steeple, are to be found today in urban areas along the eastern seaboard, around Pittsburgh and in the industrial cities of the Great Lakes region.

Chicago represents a classic study in the amazing diversity that second wave of immigration would bring to American Catholicism. In 1910, the city had ninety-three territorial parishes, thirty-five German congregations and thirty-four Polish. By the time of the First World War, nearly five thousand foreign-language parishes stood on American soil. In Chicago alone the Church ministered to twenty-eight nationalities. St. Stanislaus Kostka, the Polish mother church, was a massive institution with thousands of members, nearly seventy-five organizations, two high schools and a college.

In so vast a network of personalities and nationalities, conflicts were inevitable, especially since the hierarchy, by now overwhelmingly Irish, wanted Catholics—newcomers included—to become part of the American mainstream. The Polish community underwent strains often related to parishes' insistence on managing their own affairs and having Polish clergy—a return to the discredited trusteeism. The first separation occurred in the 1890's, culminating in 1907 in a Polish National Catholic Church.

A split among Lithuanians resulted in the formation of a separate Lithuanian National Church at Chicago in 1906. When the bishop appointed a pastor not to the liking of a Slovak parish in Bridgeport, Connecticut, one hundred women of the congregation broke into the rectory and chased the unwelcome cleric into the attic.

Inevitably, this age of Catholic expansion came to be known as the "brick and mortar" era as the institutional Church struggled to keep pace with explosive growth. Even today, quite modest neighborhoods in large cities along the Great Lakes boast massive, cathedral-like parish churches. The immigrant newcomers were generous in their support, giving to the limits of their means to build an outstanding church, an emblem of their pride and identity, of their faith and homeland. The vast Basilica of St. Josaphat that dominates the skyline of the south side of Milwaukee is one notable example.

In these national churches as well as in the more traditional territorial parishes, a popular religious event was the parish mission, the Catholic equivalent of the Protestant revival.

DAN. A. RUDD, Editor.

American Catholic Tribune,

THE · ONLY · CATHOLIC · JOURNAL · PUBLISHED · BY · COLORED · MEN · IN · AMERICA.

355 CENTRAL AVENUE, OPP. COURT,

Cincinnati, Sept 5 1888

Most Rev. Jas. Gibbons,
Cardinal Archbishop of Baltimore

Your Eminence

I write on behalf of myself and others to ask that we be permitted to hold a meeting of Colored Catholics in Washington D. C. as per the accompanying "Call". The gentlemen whose names appear thereon have expressed a strong desire for the meeting and I ask for permission to hold our convention in your Archdiocese before sending them the call for signatures.

Mt. Rev. Archbishop Elder gives his kindly approval to our undertaking and we now ask the same kind office at the hands of your Eminence.

Praying a favorable reply and asking your blessing I am yours Obedtly,

Dan. A. Rudd

P. S. Please return the call with reply.

Reply D. A. R.

Above: Daniel Rudd, the driving force behind the Black Catholic Congress. Opposite: Rudd's letter to Baltimore's Cardinal James Gibbons, requesting permission to hold a meeting of black Catholics.

Redemptorist, Paulist, Passionist and Jesuit priests crisscrossed the country to preach missions that emphasized the destructive force of sin (especially drunkenness and impurity) and the need for the sacraments. As reported in Jay Dolan's landmark study *Catholic Revivalism*, a typical mission day consisted of Mass at 5:00 a.m., followed by a series of sermons and a long period of individual confessions. Special religious books and articles were sold, and the more emotional pieties encouraged.

A burgeoning population brought with it an outburst of creative energies throughout Catholic America. A series of national Black Catholic Congresses were held, beginning at Baltimore in 1889. With former slave Daniel Rudd (1854-1933) as their driving force, the assemblies emphasized devotion, education and racial pride—all in an era when black Catholics faced humiliation and discrimination in the Church as well as in society.

Fraternal organizations arose in the these decades as well: the Knights of Columbus (1882), the Knights of St. John (1886), the Knights of Peter Claver (1909) and the Holy Name Society (1909). Women's groups included the Daughters of Isabella (1897) and the National Catholic Women's Union (1916). In many parishes across the country, the St. Vincent de Paul Society, established in the United States earlier in the century (1845), grew into a prime source of aid for those with economic difficulties.

In the political and economic realms, Catholics began to make their mark. To focus on New York City alone, the aptly named Thomas Fortune Ryan (1851-1928) rose to a position of immense wealth, eventually donating over twenty million dollars to Catholic causes. William Grace (1832-1904), owner of a steamship line, became New York City's first Catholic mayor in 1880, a political "arrival" for an entire people. Meanwhile, ward politics (political clout based on organized voting power at the precinct level) was managed by the power behind the throne at Tammany Hall, "Honest John" Kelly. In Boston and in other cities across the land, Catholics often assumed political leadership at precinct levels.

A growing array of Catholic periodicals began publication after the Civil War: *Ave Maria* (1865), *The Catholic World* (1866), *The Messenger of the Sacred Heart* (1866), *St. Anthony Messenger* (1893). The *American Ecclesiastical Review*, primarily for priests, appeared in 1889. In layman John

Gilmary Shea (1826-1892), American Catholicism found its first fully professional historian. In 1884 he formed the U.S. Catholic Historical Society, to be joined in 1919 by Peter Guilday's American Catholic Historical Association. In the Gilded Age, Catholic laywomen were involved in a wide range of activities, from the founding of welfare leagues to the establishment of labor union and temperance societies. Elizabeth Flynn Rogers (1847-1939) founded the first women's labor union in Chicago. Eva MacDonald Valesh (1874-1952), described by one historian as a "feminine comet across the political sky," spoke out for women and became an organizer for the American Federation of Labor (AFL). Mary Boyle O'Reilly (1873-1939) wrote cogently for the Boston *Pilot* and later the Boston *Globe*. Wellesley graduate and convert Marion Gurney established a settlement house for New York City's needy in 1896 and went on to found a religious community to expand settlement work among the poorest of the poor. Louise Imogene Guiney (1862-1920), a Boston essayist and poet, came to be known as one of the finer Catholic intellectuals of her age. Meanwhile labor organizer Mary Harris ("Mother") Jones (1830-1930) gave memorable advice: "Pray for the dead and fight like hell for the living."

Imogene Guiney, Boston essayist and poet, was a Catholic intellectual of the early twentieth century.

While Catholics had become the largest single religious group in the country and continued to grow in numbers and significance, they remained a minority compared to the total Protestant population of the country. (The second wave of immigration brought a large Jewish community into the American scene as well.) The Protestant community, like the Catholic, contained both conservative and liberal factions. The conservatives sought a return to fundamental biblical teaching, feared the new scriptural criticism and preached traditional messages against sin and, at times, Romanism. The liberals, such as Henry Ward Beecher, continued the mid-century mellowing theological trends and began to speak of a social gospel tradition.

The social gospel stressed the role not only of personal sin as a barrier to human progress, but of social sin as well. Thus such leaders as Walter Rauschenbusch and Washington Gladden urged believers to change the structures of society that resulted in the loss of dignity and rights for whole classes of people.

Catholics of this era, except in the area of labor relations, did not generally address the issue of systemic injustice; their energies were directed toward the absorption of immigrant peoples. And yet John Lancaster Spalding had enunciated a central Catholic tenet in his dictum that "the mission of the Church is not only to save souls, but to save society." The implications of a social theology would become readily apparent in the generations ahead, for the United States in the twentieth century was a nation increasingly in need of spiritual and moral renewal. The plaint was enshrined in a poem written by Katherine Lee Bates in 1892 that eventually became one of America's most treasured national hymns, "America the Beautiful" (1910). Its second verse, not nearly so well known as the line about purple mountain majesty, is an unabashed appeal for American reform:

America! America! God mend thine every flaw,
Confirm thy soul in self-control, thy liberty in law.

Part Four

The Twentieth Century: Innocence and Experience

Chapter Ten

New Century, New Challenges

As America entered the twentieth century, its Catholic community had become a patchwork of ethnic diversities. Even so, the common characteristics that had emerged by the turn of the century continued to mark Catholics until the Second Vatican Council:

Highly devotional. Catholics turned to a welter of emotional and expressive pieties: rosaries, novenas, processions, religious medals, scapulars and devotion to the saints.

Morally rigid and disciplined. Fasting rules applied to receiving Communion as well as to the penitential seasons of Advent and Lent. With an emphasis on personal rather than societal sin, the faithful were encouraged to careful self-scrutiny and frequent confession.

Intellectual but ambivalent. Although the majority were not well-educated, American Catholics came from a European tradition that revered the intellectual, the writer and the academy. By mid-century, they would build and sustain over three hundred colleges. Yet they were keenly aware that one of the key lessons reason could teach was its own limitation and its close proximity to the cardinal sin of pride.

Institution-building. The community was eager to leave structural marks across the continent. Churches, schools, hospitals and orphanages proliferated in this era of brick and mortar.

Insular. Catholics lived not only in ethnic neighborhoods but in a kind of ghetto served by its own schools, hospitals, newspapers, clubs, organizations and professional societies. The atmosphere was the opposite of ecumenical, especially when it came to worship or marriage with Protestants.

The people of St. Edward's in Jeffersontown, Kentucky, celebrate their parish's twenty-fifth anniversary.

A Sampler of Mid-Twentieth-Century Prayers

Prayer to St. Michael the Archangel

Holy Michael the Archangel, defend us in battle. Be our protection against the wickedness and snares of the devil. Rebuke him, O God, we humbly pray; and do thou, Prince of the divine host, by the power of God, thrust into hell Satan and all the other evil spirits who wander through the world seeking the ruin of souls.

(Recited by priest and people at the end of every Mass)

The Crusaders' Hymn

An army of youth,
Flying the standard of truth,
We're fighting for Christ, our Lord.
Heads lifted high!
Catholic Action! our cry,
And the cross our only sword.

On earth's battlefield
Ne'er a vantage we'll yield,
As undaunted on we sing.
Comrades true, dare and do,
Neath the Queen's white and blue,
For our flag, for our faith,
For Christ, our King.

(Song of the Catholic Students' Mission Crusade)

Prayer to the Guardian Angel

Angel of God, my guardian dear
To whom God's love commits me here,
Ever this day be at my side,
To light and guard, to rule and guide. Amen.

(Recited daily in Catholic schools)

Excess, intolerance and injustice could clearly occur in such an ethos. But these years also witnessed the formation of a deep legacy of faith that encouraged reverence, solemnity, sacrifice, selfless compassion, earnestness and clarity of purpose—indispensable qualities for the tasks that lay ahead.

The American Catholic community was maturing. In 1908, Rome had officially removed the Church in the United States from missionary status and accountability to the Congregation for the Propagation of the Faith in matters of faith and discipline. Within three years, the Catholic Foreign Mission Society of America (Maryknoll) was established and soon sent hundreds of its American sisters and priests to serve as missionaries in far-flung lands.

In the scholarly realm, too, there were signs of maturity. New weekly periodicals appeared, such as *America*, founded by the Jesuits in 1909, to be followed by *Commonweal*, initiated by layman Michael Williams in 1924. In 1912, the massive *Catholic Encyclopedia*, a landmark of scholarship, came off the

Agnes Repplier received high honors for her writings. Maurice Francis Egan wrote over thirty books and served in the diplomatic corps.

presses at Catholic University in Washington.

Catholic writers were increasingly busy at their craft, though none of them were to attain classic literary status. That was to be reserved for such inactive Catholics as F. Scott Fitzgerald, Ernest Hemingway and Eugene O'Neill. One of the best-known writers within the Catholic fold was Agnes Repplier (1855-1950), who had been dismissed from two schools as a rebel before she began her long career as an essayist and biographer of such figures as Jacques Marquette and Junipero Serra. She was elected to the National Institute of Arts and Letters and received Notre Dame's prestigious Laetare Medal.

Katherine Thompson Norris (1880-1966) became one of the most popular Catholic novelists, even though she adopted political positions unpopular in her time. (She opposed child labor as well as capital punishment, and later served as president of the Mothers of America, a pacifist association.) Her novels include *Angel in the House* (1933), *Beauty's Daughter* (1935) and *Lost Sunrise* (1939).

A more conservative popular novelist was Lucille Papin Borden (1873-1963), whose *Candlestick Makers* opposed birth control. Maurice Francis Egan (1852-1924), literary critic and Catholic University professor, combined the authorship of over thirty books with active international diplomatic service. His works include *The Ghost of Hamlet* (1892) and *Studies in Literature* (1899). Margaret Culkin Banning (1891-1982) produced hundreds of short stories and over forty books in her career, including *Country Club People* (1923) and *Half Loaves* (1921). Meanwhile the uncrowned poet among Catholics of this era was the soldier who died in the First World War, Joyce Kilmer (1866-1918), best known for his poem "Trees."

Despite the extensive involvement of American Catholic women in education, literature, social services and health care, a curious ambivalence persisted on the burning national issue of votes for women. As the nineteenth constitutional amendment allowing women's suffrage came closer to enactment Catholics, Cardinal Gibbons of Baltimore among them, were frequently aligned with the opposition. The American Federation of Catholic Societies pronounced the suffrage movement a menace to home and family. Prominent Catholic women leaders lined up in opposition as well, including novelist Katherine Conway (1853-1927) and labor activist Mother Jones. But Catholic women spoke out forcefully in favor of the amendment's passage as well. Jane Campbell (1845-1928) founded the Philadelphia Woman's Suffrage Association, and Margaret Foley (1875-1957), a labor leader in Boston took to heckling her opponents and dropping leaflets from a balloon.

In other areas of social concern, Catholics were highly visible. Priests such as Peter Yorke and Peter Dietz became deeply involved in the cause of labor relations. No national figure was more influential in forming the Catholic conscience on labor and social issues than Father John A. Ryan (1869-1945), a longtime professor at Catholic University. His 1906 study *A Living Wage*, based on the social justice teaching of Pope Leo XIII, became a landmark text in the ethics of economics.

Another academic and priest at Catholic University, sociologist William Kerby (1870-1936), was responsible for the 1910 formation of the National Conference of Catholic Charities, whose task was the professionalization and expansion of the Church's outreach to those in need. Ten years later, the National Conference of Catholic Men and the National Conference of Catholic Women were established to intensify religious and civic action among the laity. With an eye to bettering the condition of the often-forgotten farmer, Father Edwin O'Hara was instrumental in 1923 in the formation of the National Catholic Rural Life Conference.

With America's entry into the First World War in 1917,

For Discussion

Is enthusiastic support for a war a good measure of patriotism? Why or why not?

Catholics trooped to the colors in record numbers. The one million Catholics in the armed forces constituted over twenty percent of the U.S. military, more than Catholic percentages in the population. Out of some four thousand conscientious objectors to the war, only four were of the Catholic faith. Catholics of this era were pleased to cite such figures. They considered them a proof of patriotism in those days when Catholics were still considered somehow "foreign" to the American scene.

The world conflict itself was proclaimed by national leaders to be the war to end all wars. The Great War was widely viewed in America as a tragic fact but an ongoing step on the road to human progress. Catholic publications found themselves caught up in the enthusiasm as well. The Louisville *Record* declared that the week of the armistice was the "greatest...since the days of Calvary," one that foreshadowed a new order of human civilization.

For those whose political sentiments ran to the progressive, the years at the war's end were a heady time. In 1918, Congress passed the Eighteenth Amendment, which brought prohibition to the land. While a great many Catholics opposed the action, it was also true that the movement for total temperance and "the pledge" had been a prominent feature for decades in some Catholic circles, especially among the Irish. Just as some naively thought that the problems associated with alcoholism were eradicated by prohibition, so many came to believe that granting votes to women in 1920 would put an end to the second-class status of women in American life.

The year after the armistice, 1919, witnessed an important development in the structure of the Church in America. In that year, the war-generated National Catholic War Council was given continued life and rechristened the National Catholic Welfare Conference. The new organization created for laity and clerics alike a major network to foster social and political change.

In its debut year, the NCWC released a moral and political bombshell. Known as the "Bishops' Program of Social Reconstruction," this document—largely the brainchild of John A. Ryan—was the first major statement by the Catholic prelates of the United States on social and economic issues. The Program helped to place the American hierarchy in the vanguard among those in the Church worldwide who

Hymns to the Blessed Virgin Mary

Mother Dear, O Pray for Me

Mother dear, O pray for me
Whilst far from heaven and thee,
I wander in a fragile bark
O'er life's tempestuous sea.

Mother dear, remember me
And never cease thy care
Till in heaven eternally
Thy love and bliss I share.

On This Day, O Beautiful Mother

On this day, O beautiful Mother,
On this day, we give thee our love,
Near thee, Madonna, fondly we hover,
Trusting thy gentle care to prove.

On this day, we hope to share,
Dearest Mother, thy sweet care.
Lead us, ere our feet astray,
Wander from thy guiding way.

The Protestant Social Gospel Tradition

Since God is in it, the Kingdom of God is always both present and future. Like God it is in all tenses, eternal in the midst of time. It is the energy of God realizing itself in human life. Its future lies among the mysteries of God. It invites and justifies prophecy....

It is for us to see the Kingdom of God as always coming, always pressing on the present, always big with possibility, and always inviting immediate action. We walk by faith. Every human life is so placed that it can share with God in the creation of the Kingdom, or can resist and retard its progress. The Kingdom is for each of us the supreme task and the supreme gift of God. (Walter Rauschenbusch)

specifically linked political and social action to the gospel mandates. It was the forerunner of such major documents as the pastoral letters on peace and on the economy in the 1980's. It called for sweeping changes in the government's role in order to improve the social condition of the people.

The bishops' proposals advocated labor's right to organize and bargain collectively, as well as government-backed insurance to protect against unemployment, illness, accident and old age. Many of these proposals would not be enacted into law until the New Deal years. Meanwhile, in some quarters the prelates earned for themselves the unflattering nickname of "the red bishops."

The rising tide of Catholic presence and influence was not to pass without opposition. The old Puritan ways of smugness, intolerance and moral stricture had never entirely died away. In the late nineteenth century, as massive immigration continued unabated, some Protestant leaders had been terrified at what they perceived as the twin dangers of Catholic growth and modern atheistic thought. Professor Russell Hitchcock summarized such fears in 1873 in his assertion that "infidel bugles are blowing in front of us; papal bugles are sounding behind."

The American Protective Association (APA) came into being in 1887 to counter the growth of immigrant power in America. From 1915 onward, a renewed Ku Klux Klan turned its attention toward Catholics as well as blacks and Jews. In the 1920's, Florida Governor Sidney Catts averred that the pope was planning an invasion of his state. Oregon passed a law in 1922 requiring all children to attend public schools, only to see its efforts overturned by the United States Supreme Court in 1925.

For those of a fundamentalist stripe, the 1920's were an active time. The 1925 Scopes "Monkey Trial" in Dayton, Tennessee, focused attention on the question of teaching evolution in the schools.

National agitation over religious issues heated again in 1928, when the Democratic Party nominated the Catholic governor of New York, Alfred Emanuel Smith (1873-1944), as a candidate for president of the United States. This unprecedented political choice drew forth long-simmering anti-Catholic feeling across the land. In the election, Smith was thoroughly trounced by the Republican candidate, Herbert

For Discussion

The Bishops' Program of Social
Reconstruction was the first such
statement on social and political
realities. Should the bishops be
writing about such things? Why or
why not?

Hoover. For the first time since the Civil War, about half of the states of the "solid South," which had always voted Democratic, turned their electoral allegiance to the Republicans. While a heavy dose of the opposition to Smith was surely due to fear of Catholic power, other factors made his election unlikely in any event. "Republican prosperity" remained strong in 1928, and any Democratic candidate would have had an uphill climb. Additionally, Al Smith was a "wet," opposing prohibition in a nation that still believed in its value.

When over 35,000 Ku Klux Klansmen paraded their strength down Washington's Pennsylvania Avenue in 1925, many Americans sat up and took notice. But a parade along Michigan Avenue in Chicago the following year raised eyebrows as well—of those who feared that Catholics were becoming too visible in American life and culture. For the first time an American diocese, Chicago, was hosting an International Eucharistic Congress.

In the Michigan Avenue cavalcade rode nine cardinals of the Roman Catholic Church, both European and American, resplendent in their red robes. These eminent visitors had descended on the midwestern metropolis from New York on a special train painted red for the occasion. For five days,

Crowds assemble at Soldier Field for the International Eucharistic Congress in Chicago, 1926.

Catholics from across America made a public display of their eucharistic faith. A Mass at Soldier Field drew some one hundred fifty thousand people. The finale took place above the city at St. Mary of the Lake (now popularly called Mundelein) Seminary, a grandiose institution opened only five years earlier. Nearly half a million knelt on rain-soaked ground as the final Benediction of the Blessed Sacrament took place.

The massive display in Chicago, under the direction of Cardinal George Mundelein (1872-1939), was indicative of the new style in the American Catholic Church. A people who had once been content to practice their faith quietly, Catholics after World War I had attained sufficient self-confidence to take public pride in their presence and their distinctive religious style.

This pride was augmented by that fact that the Vatican had appointed in several major archdioceses Roman-trained archbishops, who ruled their domains with a lordly sense of power. In addition to Mundelein, the most notable of these prelates were William Henry O'Connell of Boston (1859-1944) and Dennis Dougherty of Philadelphia (1865-1951). All these men were named cardinals, "princes of the Church," by Rome, and they clearly took their royal designations seriously. Only two American archbishops had been named cardinals in the entire nineteenth century: John McCloskey of New York in 1875 and James Gibbons of Baltimore in 1886. The rash of new cardinals early in the century signified yet again the growing significance of American Catholicism in the universal Church.

Mundelein, Dougherty and O'Connell all subscribed to the idea of a highly organized, disciplined and hierarchical Church. In Philadelphia, Cardinal Dougherty had once exhorted his faithful to boycott all movies currently playing in order to persuade Hollywood to make purer films. In an oration at his silver jubilee, he had summarized his Roman proclivities with the dictum: "After God, I owe what I am to the Holy See."

To American Catholicism in the early and middle years of the twentieth century, such adjectives as *pious*, *vigorous*, *assertive* or *defensive* could all be aptly applied. But more recent historians, following the lead of a pivotal study by William Halsey, have concentrated on yet another descriptive term: *innocent*. Increasingly aware of the disbelief and detachment from traditional morality in the modern world, Catholics consciously and deliberately established an enclave

Cardinal George Mundelein was every inch a prince of the Church, ruling the Archdiocese of Chicago with lordly power.

For Discussion

Interview someone who can recall the flavor of Catholic life in the mid-twentieth century or before. Compare Catholic devotion then and now. What are the similarities? How significant are the differences?

of protection within their Church. This "ghetto mentality" involved not only separate Catholic schools, youth groups and professional societies, but also distinctive practices that set Catholics apart from their culture—Ash Wednesday ashes, fish on Fridays, Saturday confession.

It was not a Catholic, though, but essayist Walter Lippmann who most chillingly sounded the alarm of modern disillusionment and disarray in a 1929 classic, *A Preface to Morals*. Using chapter headings such as "Whirl is King," "The Acids of Modernity" and "The Breakdown of Authority," Lippmann sounded the alarm over the "dissolution of the ancestral order." In the face of such a threat, Catholics were not the only religious people to try perpetuating the ancient order.

Even so, by virtue of their faith, size, philosophy, centralized organization and insular culture, Catholics were in a singular position. Theirs was a dialectical faith that sought, sometimes shakily, to balance tradition with modernity, faith with reason, law with spirit, the individual with the community. They felt it their duty and call to safeguard an innocence associated not only with the virtues of Christianity but with the foundational values of the American republic as well.

In this task, Catholics were guided by Christian humanism, with its appeal to reason and natural law and its abiding trust in human possibility. As historian William Halsey phrased it in *The Survival of American Innocence*: "When Catholics peered at the universe, they saw, not flux and contingency, but order, harmony and law."

Here is to be seen the drama of history at its most ironic. At the outset of the twentieth century, many an American was to consider Catholicism the leading threat to the maintenance of the American republic. Within a generation, a growing number of Catholics had begun to regard their faith and life-style as primary forces helping to hold the nation together in the storm of modern disconnection. As the century progressed, the crisis of change was to become more, not less, intense.

Chapter Eleven

Global War and
Troubled Peace

On the morning of March 4, 1933, the inauguration day of
Franklin D. Roosevelt as America's thirty-second president, his
predecessor Herbert Hoover confided to an aide: "We are at the
end of our string." The country was, in fact, in economic chaos;
Roosevelt later made the startling comment that he saw
one-third of the nation ill-housed and ill-fed.

In those dark days, American Catholics, largely a working-
class population, became strong supporters of Roosevelt's New
Deal. They were by and large the economic class the New Deal
set out primarily to serve, and the Roosevelt program fit closely
with the Catholic social teachings of the popes, most notably
Leo XIII and Pius XI. Father John A. Ryan, whose thought had
shaped the bishops' social statement of 1919 (see pp. 122, 124)
was so close to the administration that he was asked to offer the
benediction at two Roosevelt inaugurations. In a *Commonweal*
article of October 1934, Ryan observed: "Never before in our
history have the policies of the federal government embodied
so much legislation that is of a highly ethical order."

Many Catholic clerics shared Ryan's enthusiasm and
energies, especially in the area of labor relations. Among these
were Archbishop John T. McNicholas of Cincinnati and Father
Raymond McGowan, Director of the Social Action Department
of the National Catholic Welfare Conference. In terms of
numbers, though, it was the laity, working men and women,
who formed the great bulk of Catholic involvement in the labor
movement. The Association of Catholic Trade Unionists
(ACTU), formed in 1937, soon had chapters in fourteen cities.
In industrial Detroit, over twenty-five hundred ACTU members
were in place by 1941. The leadership of the Association not
only encouraged workers to join unions and to strike when

*The atomic bombs dropped on
Hiroshima and (left) Nagasaki in
August 1945 signaled the end of
World War II and the beginning
of the Cold War.*

necessary; they also maintained a mighty struggle to keep racketeers and Communists out of labor circles.

Catholics had been highly visible in the American Federation of Labor, organized in 1886. When the Congress of Industrial Organizations (CIO) came into existence in 1938, three Catholics were on the executive board, including layman Philip Murray, who became CIO president after 1940. In this era, historians estimate, some thirty percent of membership in the industrial unions and forty percent of the leadership were Catholics. The full effectiveness of Catholicism in the American labor movement has yet to be fully evaluated. But it is clear that the Church aided immeasurably in making unions a readily accepted force in American life, in bettering the working and living conditions of millions of workers and in helping to purge disruptive forces from within the unions themselves.

Across the nation, lay Catholics helped to spark an unprecedented burst of religious and social justice activism. This dynamic new lay action was America's contribution to a worldwide lay revival. It incorporated the best of Christian humanism in its effort to revivify society. Leading philosophers of the movement were lay French philosophers Jacques Maritain (1882-1973) and Raissa Maritain (1883-1960), who came to live in the United States in 1940.

The new activism also reflected a theology of social justice and Catholic Action energetically put forth in the pronouncements of Pope Pius XI. American hometown experience and papal teaching joined together to shape the new direction in American Catholicism in at least two other areas: (1) an appreciation that all members of the Church are part of Christ's Mystical Body, enunciated in Pope Pius XII's 1943 encyclical *Mystici Corporis* and (2) a deepening liturgical renewal stressing Scripture and sacrament, rooted in the work of Benedictine Virgil Michel (1890-1938) at Collegeville, Minnesota, and articulated in Pius's 1947 encyclical *Mediator Dei*. (The liturgical renewal, however, was far from widespread; its impact would not be generally felt until the time of the Second Vatican Council in the 1960's.)

A new catalog of movements and organizations appeared on the Catholic American landscape. Historian Patrick Carey offers a partial listing: "Michael Williams' *Commonweal* (1924), Peter Maurin and Dorothy Day's Catholic Worker

Movement (1933), Catherine de Hueck Doherty's Friendship Houses,...Pat and Patty Crowley's Christian Family Movement (1947), the Grail Movement, Cana Conferences, Catholic Youth Organization, Young Catholic Students, Young Christian Workers." All of these, writes Carey, represented "predominantly elite lay movements to Christianize modern culture."

The Chicago area in particular was the scene of intense lay and clerical energies. The consecration of Bernard Sheil (1886-1969) as auxiliary bishop in 1928 helped to trigger enthusiasm, for Sheil was soon vigorously active: founding the Catholic Youth Organization (CYO) with its religious and

Children play under Sister's watchful eye at the CYO Vacation Center, Chicago.

Dorothy Day's Challenge

My criticism of Christians in the past, and it still holds good of too many of them, is that they in fact deny God and reject Him. "Amen, I say to you, as long as you did it to one of these my least brethren, you did it to me" (Matthew 25:40), Christ said, and today there are Christians who affront Christ in the Negro, in the poor Mexican, the Italian, yes, and the Jew. Catholics believe that man is the temple of the Holy Ghost, that he is made in the image and likeness of God. We believe that of Jew and Gentile. We believe that all men are members or potential members of the Mystical Body of Christ and since there is no time with God, we must so consider each man whether he is atheist, Jew or Christian.

You ask do we really believe it, when we see our fellows herded like brutes in municipal lodging houses, tramping the streets and roads hungry, working at starvation wages or under an inhuman speed-up, living in filthy degrading conditions. Seeing many Christians denying Him in the poor, is it any wonder a heresy has sprung up denying Him in words and deed? (*From Union Square to Rome*)

social emphasis; supporting the CIO; helping form the Back of the Yards Neighborhood Council to empower people through education and political activity, and working for racial equality as well. Chicago seminary rector Father Raymond Hillenbrand (1904-1979) instilled in his students an informed passion for excellence in liturgy and justice in the community. In the later 1940's, the Christian Family Movement was formed in Chicago. It insisted on strong lay leadership and laid special emphasis on the linkage between the family and society at large.

No lay movement in American Catholic history so consistently struck a countercultural chord as that of the Catholic Worker, founded in New York City in 1933 by Dorothy Day (1897-1980) and Peter Maurin (1877-1949). Day, a former Communist and a convert to Catholicism, turned her

Dorothy Day (right) meets with the Catholic Worker *staff in September 1934.*

considerable energies to the care of the poorest of the poor in Catholic Worker houses across the country. Hers was a radical vision that urged voluntary poverty, lively intellectual and literary life, traditional prayer and sacramental life, total pacifism and activism for greater justice in American life.

Day's special concern for addressing racism in the nation found substantial—though far from unanimous—support in her co-religionists. This was an era when "white only" signs stood on public facilities in the South—and in the pews of some Catholic churches as well. Not only in the South, but throughout America, black citizens were subjected to systematic exclusion from educational, social and career opportunities and to a long list of indignities.

An early pioneer who set out to shape the Catholic conscience in new directions on the racial question was Jesuit

John LaFarge (1880-1963). LaFarge was involved in the formation of the first Catholic Interracial Council in 1934, and saw the creation of the National Catholic Conference for Interracial Justice at the 1958 convention in Chicago.

Some Catholic bishops, most notably Archbishop Joseph Ritter in St. Louis in 1947, integrated their diocesan schools long before a 1954 Supreme Court decision moved public schools in the same direction.

For Discussion

Anti-Semitism like Father Charles Coughlin's helped to form a climate of hate. What happens when societies harbor hatred? To what extent do such feelings toward Jews or other groups still exist in the United States? In your parish? What solutions do you see?

Meanwhile, black Catholics themselves found new voices. Howard University professor Thomas Wyatt Turner (1877-1978) was a key figure in the founding of the Federated Colored Catholics, which resisted discrimination in Catholic parishes and institutions. The 1920's explosion of culture known as the Harlem Renaissance produced such black Catholic literary leaders as Ellen Tarry (b. 1906) and Claude McKay (1890-1948).

The 1930's brought American Catholics into highly public view in two controversies: the immense political popularity of radio preacher Father Charles Coughlin, and the Church's attitude toward the Spanish Civil War. Coughlin (1891-1979), a Detroit priest, began a radio career on that city's station WJR. The program soon was picked up by CBS; his radio listeners were eventually estimated at some forty million. The fiery Coughlin had begun as a supporter of the New Deal, only to turn into one of Roosevelt's most outspoken critics. The preacher's rhetoric endeared him to millions, but his personal sympathies would eventually take him down the road of anti-Semitism. As his sympathies for fascist leaders in Europe became more pronounced, Coughlin complied with an order from Archbishop Edward Mooney of Detroit taking him off the air.

The Spanish Civil War (1936-1939), often considered a preliminary round of the Second World War, squared off fascist-friendly Francisco Franco and his Nationalists against the Republicans, who received support from Moscow. Under the Second Republic, established after the fall of the monarchy in 1931, convents were burned, Church property confiscated and the Jesuits dissolved. Anti-Catholic fury intensified and, by the war's end, resulted in the deaths of nearly 7,000 priests and three hundred sisters, as well as countless laypeople.

Tensions in the United States ran high over the conflict, with Catholics registering strong support for the Franco forces.

Catholic periodicals, almost without exception, trumpeted the Nationalist cause. A Gallup poll of late 1938, in fact, found American Catholics fifty-eight percent pro-Franco, compared to only seventeen percent of their Protestant neighbors.

By 1940, the Catholic population of the United States had reached twenty-one million. Catholic Frank Murphy, who had served briefly as the nation's attorney general, was appointed by Roosevelt that same year to the "Catholic seat" on the Supreme Court, a tradition dating back to 1894. In the following year, 1941, the American Catholic bishops issued a pastoral letter, *The Crisis of Christianity*, noting the threat posed to the world by Nazism on the political right and Communism on the left: "Christianity faces today its most serious crisis since the church came out of the catacombs." The bishops also welcomed the bishop of a new diocese into their midst in September 1941: the Diocese of Honolulu. In it was located the American base at Pearl Harbor.

After the Japanese attack on Pearl Harbor December 7,

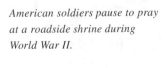

American soldiers pause to pray at a roadside shrine during World War II.

1941, the United States entered the second global war of the century. Catholics constituted over twenty-five percent of the armed forces. Many parishes displayed special honor rolls listing members who had fallen in battle. Catholics partook generally of the patriotic intensity of the war years. Yet, at times during the conflict Catholic ethicists raised moral questions about certain military actions: the saturation bombing of civilian populations in enemy cities (such as Dresden), the destruction of the ancient abbey of Monte Casino in Italy and the dropping of the first atomic bombs. After the Hiroshima bombing, Father James Gillis, editor of *The Catholic World*, declared that the United States was responsible for "the most powerful blow ever delivered against Christian civilization and moral law." Meanwhile, polls indicated that over half of the American Catholic rank and file

Radio and television brought popular speaker Bishop Fulton J. Sheen into both Catholic and Protestant homes.

approved using the nuclear devices.

For Discussion

Discuss the morality of saturation bombing and nuclear weapons.

One result of the Second World War, little remarked at the time, foreshadowed an enormous change in the texture of American Catholicism: the G.I. Bill of Rights, which permitted veterans to attend college at government expense. Hundreds of thousands of Catholic veterans soon found themselves on state university campuses, far from the "Catholic ghetto," exposed to a vast pluralism of faith and ideas. Coupled with the gradual social and economic rise of Catholics in the culture, the G.I. Bill may have been a force for change in the American Church rivaled only by the documents of the Second Vatican Council.

A benevolent (some might say insipid) image of Catholicism—especially of sisters and priests—had been spread across the movie screens of the United States in such minor film classics as *Going My Way* (1944) and *The Bells of St. Mary's* (1945). Even so, Catholicism in the 1940's and 1950's found itself embroiled in civic and political controversies that even the sweetness of Ingrid Bergman's Mother Superior or the grumpy kindness of Barry Fitzgerald as an Irish pastor could not easily cast aside.

The number of Catholics was manifestly growing. Conversions were increasing, including such famous figures as journalist Heywood Broun, Clare Booth Luce (later ambassador to Italy) and Thomas Merton, whose 1948 autobiography *The Seven-Storey Mountain* became a runaway best-seller. Bishop Fulton J. Sheen (1895-1979) had become an enormously popular writer, as well as a radio and later television speaker who appealed to Protestant and Catholic alike. He was even said to have run a media ratings race with the popular comedian Milton Berle; listeners had to choose between Uncle Miltie and Uncle Fultie. In short, Catholicism had assumed a new national popularity. But the old national fears of a powerful Catholicism were quick to follow.

In 1947, Protestants and Other Americans United for the Separation of Church and State (P.O.A.U.) was formed. Two years later, Paul Blanshard, a leader of P.O.A.U. had a best-seller of his own when he sounded an alarm on rising Catholic strength in his *American Freedom and Catholic Power*. In these years, mine fields seemed to appear everywhere in Church-State relations: Presidents Roosevelt and Truman sent diplomatic representatives to the Vatican. The U.S. Supreme Court in the 1947 decision *Everson v. Board of*

Education approved the use of public school buses to carry Catholic students to parochial schools.

Within the intellectual circles of American Catholicism, the Church-State issue touched off a ferocious debate between Father Joseph Fenton, editor of *American Ecclesiastical Review*, and Jesuit Father John Courtney Murray (1904-1967), editor of *Theological Studies*, a journal which had appeared in 1940. Fenton represented an older, more conservative theological approach that feared too much mingling of Catholics and Protestants and maintained that the ideal Church-State arrangement was a Catholic commonwealth. He granted that, in current American conditions, this would be an impossibility; compromises would have to be accepted.

Murray, much beleaguered at the time, represented the party of the future, for his approach would eventually be accepted in the Second Vatican Council's *Declaration on Religious Liberty*. Murray taught, according to historian James Hennesey, "that the one requirement of the state for the Church was freedom; his explanation of the human right to religious freedom started from the assertion of individual human dignity and its necessary consequences."

Murray, long constrained by his superiors from writing on this sensitive topic, continued to reject a growing secularism Hennesey describes as "built on destroying the traditional concept of man and setting in its place a positive new ideal—a humanism without God." Later Murray would elaborate his political commentary in a 1960 study entitled *We Hold These Truths*. America's most fundamental political principles, he insisted, were grounded in the natural law and strikingly in tune with traditional Catholic thought.

Once again, a great irony was to be found in the fears of those who suspected Catholicism was a sinister power aiming to undermine the nation. Few groups in America were more patriotic than Roman Catholics. No more outspoken booster of the nation was to be found than New York's Cardinal Francis Spellman (1889-1967), a man occasionally called, with slight irreverence, "the American pope." As early as 1946, Spellman told a rally at New York's Polo Grounds that Communists were "digging deep inroads into our nation." In the 1950's conservative Catholic intellectuals such as William F. Buckley, Garry Wills, John Luckas, L. Brent Bozzell and Russell Kirk were among the most vocal Americans sounding alarms about

Cardinal Francis Spellman of New York, the "American pope."

For Disussion

Interview someone who remembers the McCarthy era. Discuss the effect of paranoia on political climate, citing current examples, if you see any.

relativism, excessive optimism, irreligion and nonchalance in the face of totalitarianism.

A much more extreme brand of conservatism was to surface in the tortured political career of the Catholic senator from Wisconsin, Joseph McCarthy (1908-1957). In 1950, McCarthy galvanized the nation with his accusation that the State Department was seriously infiltrated with Communists. Within the next four years, until his condemnation by the Senate, McCarthy slashed not only at Washington officials, but at New York intellectuals and Hollywood stars and screenwriters as well. Catholic support for McCarthy, according to polls, stayed slightly ahead of that of Protestants, while Catholic journals divided their allegiance. *America* and *Commonweal* surfaced as strong opponents of the Wisconsin senator. Some of the larger diocesan papers—among them Brooklyn's *Tablet* and Los Angeles's *The Tidings*—were outspoken in the senator's defense.

Within the Catholic community itself, another controversy erupted over historian Monsignor John Tracy Ellis's 1955 essay "American Catholics and the Intellectual Life." Ellis bemoaned the disparity between America's high Catholic numbers and wealth on the one hand, and what he perceived as low Catholic intellectual leadership and achievement on the other. When Catholic universities across the nation—such as Notre Dame under the leadership of Father Theodore Hesburgh—later made concerted drives toward greater academic excellence, echoes of the Ellis critique may still have been ringing in professorial ears.

The quality of writing in the Catholic community took a decided upward turn after the Second World War. Lay professor and editor George Shuster (1894-1977), a critic of Franco and McCarthy alike, an accomplished intellectual and author of over twenty books, once argued that most Catholic fiction before World War I had been "unintelligent and unreadable." The same was not to be said of the generation that followed. Catholic writers honed their skills and became increasingly critical of their own community.

Two novelists especially influenced by contemporary developments in Catholic social thought were Henry Sylvester (best known for *Moon Gaffney* in 1947), and Joseph Dever (*No Lasting Home*, 1947). Insightful and realistic fictional portraits of Catholic clerics began to appear from the pen of J. F. Powers

Thomas Merton on the Human Condition

I love beer, and by that very fact, the world.... This is simply the voice of a self-questioning human person who, like all his brothers, struggles to cope with turbulent, mysterious, demanding, exciting, frustrating, confused existence in which almost nothing is really predictable, in which most definitions, explanations and justifications become incredible even before they are uttered, in which people suffer together and are sometimes utterly beautiful, at other times impossibly pathetic. In which almost everything public is patently phony, and in which there is at the same time an immense ground of personal authenticity that is right there and so obvious that no one can talk about it and most cannot even believe it is there. (From "Is the World a Problem?" in *Contemplation in a World of Action*)

I t is a glorious destiny to be a member of the human race, though it is a race dedicated to many absurdities and one which makes many terrible mistakes: yet, with all that, God...gloried in becoming a member of the human race. A member of the human race! To think that such a commonplace realization should suddenly seem like news that one holds the winning ticket in a cosmic sweepstake.

I have the immense joy of being...a member of a race in which God Himself became incarnate. As if the sorrows and stupidities of the human condition could overwhelm me, now I realize what we all are. And if only everybody could realize this! But it cannot be explained. There is no way of telling people that they are all walking around shining like the sun. (From *Conjectures of a Guilty Bystander*)

in his 1947 collection *Prince of Darkness*. No Catholic fiction writer of this era is more celebrated than Flannery O'Connor (1925-1964). A Southern original, she managed in books such as *Wise Blood* and *Everything That Rises Must Converge* to blend the horrific with the action of grace. In poetry, the best-known Catholic voice in wider national circles was Robert

Lowell, while in Catholic circles, the writings of Sister Mary Madeleva Wolff were widely read.

In the realm of spirituality, the writings of Thomas Merton (1915-1968), a Trappist monk of Kentucky's Gethsemani Abbey, achieved an unprecedented readership among Catholics and non-Catholics alike. Called by some the American Augustine, Merton was a Columbia University educated intellectual who became Catholic in 1938. Merton became internationally known for his religious profundity, dedication to Catholic tradition and sensitive openness to the modern world. In over a score of major works, he emerged, according to his front-page obituary in *The New York Times*, as "a writer of singular grace about the City of God and an essayist of penetrating originality on the City of Man."

Merton's writings covered a wide spectrum of spirituality, enriched not only by Catholic and monastic tradition, but by ecumenical and Oriental insights as well. In addition to producing a large collection of essays on contemporary literature, the Trappist monk railed against smugness and narrowness in the Churches. From the late 1950's on, he also lifted his pen against racism, the Vietnam War and nuclear weapons. A strong advocate of Catholic theological and liturgical renewal in the 1960's, he was also quite capable of criticizing what he considered imprecise thought and mindless change in the post-conciliar Church.

When the year 1960 dawned, the massive population of Catholics in America was clearly a community of vitality, upward social and economic mobility and considerable civic involvement. According to Flannery O'Connor, it was also afflicted with a certain besetting smugness.

By year's end, Catholic America would witness the election—by a very narrow margin—of John Fitzgerald Kennedy (1915-1963) as America's first Catholic president. With Kennedy's election, an invisible barrier had been shattered. Across the nation, Catholics sensed that they had finally achieved unquestioned first-class status as loyal citizens. Meanwhile, in Rome, intensive planning was underway for a worldwide ecumenical council, summoned by Pope John XXIII in 1959. In this heady time of the two Johns—president and pope—American Catholics stood poised on the verge of the greatest transformation in their long history—over four centuries—on North America's shores.

John Fitzgerald Kennedy, the first Catholic president.

Chapter Twelve

Diversity and Complexity

The Second Vatican Council, which met in Rome from 1962 to 1965, marked an epochal moment of historical change—not just for worldwide Catholicism, but for the Church in America as well. Alongside the bishops in attendance from the United States (among them such leaders as Albert Meyer of Chicago, Joseph Elmer Ritter of St. Louis and Paul Hallinan of Atlanta) was a galaxy of American Catholic and Protestant scholars serving as consultants. One official woman auditor had been invited from the United States as well: Sister of Loretto Mary Luke Tobin.

By the special intervention of Cardinal Spellman, the once controversial Jesuit John Courtney Murray attended as an expert on the subject of Church-State relations. His influence would be especially evident in the landmark *Declaration on Religious Liberty*, which has been widely hailed as the major contribution of American Catholicism to the worldwide Church. Especially in the areas of Scripture, liturgy and interfaith relations, American advisers would be able to bring to the assembly not only their scholarly expertise, but practical American experience as well.

In its sixteen documents, the Second Vatican Council breathed optimism about the human condition. The Council deemed the modern era to be a time of both unparalleled possibility and unprecedented peril. Quick to encourage and slow to condemn, Vatican II envisioned a renewed Church capable of nurturing the grace and goodness with which God had seeded the world.

In their theological method, the bishops of the Council moved away from tight scholasticism and legalism, taking what some observers have called a "hermeneutical turn." This means that their understanding of dogma, revelation and tradition would be enriched—though certainly not totally determined—

The bishops of the world take their seats in St. Peter's for the opening of the Second Vatican Council.

141

by modern scriptural, historical and scientific study. Several themes predominated throughout the entire Council, and all profoundly affected the Church in the United States over the next generation. These themes included:

Priority of vision. After generations of theological battles, the pivotal doctrines on which most Christians agree—such as Incarnation, Trinity, Resurrection and the Redemption—should have pride of place in the gospel proclamation.

Ecumenism. Since there is more that unites Christians than divides them, Catholics should be nurtured by prayer and dialogue with other Christians and people of other faiths. They should strive to bring the integrity of their own tradition to every such encounter.

Humility. The Church acknowledged that it is and always remains a community that falls away from its ideals. It has been at times arrogant, unjust and sinful. Always in need of reform, the Church should welcome honest evaluation and self-scrutiny, and appreciate critics who are loving as well as loyal.

Social justice. For the gospel to be preached effectively, human dignity, rights and justice must be proclaimed. Beyond proclamation, believers must be involved in the struggle to produce a better society.

Religious freedom. Because of the nature of God-given human dignity, no one may ever be coerced in matters of faith. Believers have the right to religious expression, even though they be minorities in their lands.

Liturgy. The liturgy is at the heart of Christian life, and its treasures must be made more generously available and articulate. The Council stressed (1) the centrality of the Eucharist and the great mysteries encoded in the seasonal cycles; (2) the use of vernacular language and active congregational involvement; (3) the riches of Scripture, hence an expanded cycle of readings.

Participation. There must be a sharing of ministry and greater participation in the leadership of the Church from across a wide spectrum: from the collegiality of bishops to lay involvement in parish councils.

In the United States, the conciliar years were a time of unprecedented vitality and expectation, dampened only by the tragic assassination of President Kennedy in November 1963. Even in this national calamity, Catholicism made an impact on the nation. The televised funeral allowed Catholic symbols to

For Discussion

From your own memory or from interviews, describe the impact of Vatican II on ordinary Catholics' lives. Would you describe it as positive, negative or mixed? Why?

Pope Paul VI leaves the United Nations after his 1965 address.

help unify and heal the entire nation.

In the American political arena, Catholics vaulted into the corridors of power. In the generation after 1960, over twenty-five Catholics were appointed to the presidential cabinet, compared to only six in the first one hundred fifty years of the Republic. By 1965 Catholics had become, for the first time, the largest religious group represented in the U.S. Congress, with well over one hundred members. In 1984 Catholic Geraldine Ferraro, a Democrat, became the first woman to run as a major party vice-presidential candidate.

In October 1965, Pope Paul VI arrived in New York City to address the United Nations—the first time a reigning pontiff set foot on American soil. But the Mass he celebrated in Yankee Stadium may well have marked the end of the easy euphoria at the Council's end. For the years that followed, for all their accomplishment and postconciliar zest, also proved to be a time of confusion and conflict.

While a broad majority of Catholics were generally pleased with new developments in their Church, polarities arose between those on the left who expected more rapid and fundamental transformations and those on the right who felt that Catholics were losing their distinctive traditions along with reverence and discipline. The former often found support for their views in reading the *National Catholic Reporter*; the latter, in the pages of *The Wanderer*.

The forty million Catholics in the country in 1960 were accustomed to seemingly endless institutional growth. Suddenly, within four years of the Council's conclusion, over three thousand American clerics had resigned from the priesthood. While the numbers of Catholics themselves continued to rise, figures in other categories showed a marked decrease over the next generation. A comparative chart drawn from *The Official Catholic Directory* (1961) and the 1992 *Catholic Almanac* dramatically makes the point:

	1961	1991
Catholic population	42,104,900	55,646,713
Priests	54,682	52,124
Permanent Deacons	0	9,723
Seminarians	41,871	6,266
Sisters	170,438	100,334
Brothers	10,928	6,835
Hospitals	814	636
Elementary schools	10,593	7,353
Elementary pupils	4,389,779	1,936,344
Secondary schools	2,433	1,298
Secondary pupils	886,295	603,520

If traditional forms of Catholic life were in numerical decline, great growth and vitality occurred in new directions in the postconciliar years. Most immediately apparent to ordinary churchgoers were liturgical innovations: Mass in English (beginning in 1964) with the priest facing the congregation; new forms of congregational singing and frequent "guitar

Masses"; Saturday anticipation of the Sunday obligation (1970); lay readers (1970) and eucharistic ministers (1973); Communion in the hand (1977). Other postconciliar changes included offering the cup to the faithful, the option of face-to-face confession and communal penance services, and a more ecumenical approach to interfaith marriages. Polls generally showed such changes to have wide support among the faithful. Especially popular was the 1966 ruling that permitted eating meat on non-Lenten Fridays.

If the quarter-century before the Council can be said to have been the apex of *institutional* Catholicism, the quarter-century after its conclusion witnessed the rise of *participational* Catholicism. A typical diocese in the new era of flow-chart Catholicism established over two dozen new commissions, councils and boards. These often included a diocesan pastoral council; clerical and religious senates; commissions concerned with black ministries, continuing education, due process, ecumenical affairs, evangelization, family relations, finance, lay ministries, liturgy, media, social justice, spirituality, vocations and youth ministry.

A key factor in all this organizational intensity was the rise of lay involvement on parish councils, teaching staffs, liturgical and social service ministries, as well as on the many new commissions. In addition, a permanent diaconate was established in 1967. Nearly ten thousand such ministers, many of them married men, now serve across the country.

While such innovations were aborning in the late 1960's, American Catholics found themselves embroiled in two immense debates touching the conscience of the nation—civil rights and the Vietnam conflict—and in an intramural battle over birth control that convulsed the Church's own inner life. The civil rights movement, with the Baptist minister Martin Luther King, Jr., as prime national leader, sought to remedy centuries of racial injustice and indignity. Across the country, many Catholics walked in protest marches alongside Protestant and Jewish citizens. Support was not unanimous: On some occasions, habited nuns and clergy were pelted with rocks and eggs by fellow Catholics for their participation. As urban renewal displaced black ghettos and blacks moved to previously all-white neighborhoods, many Catholics joined in the national flight to suburban areas.

But together enough religious people, black and white, lay

A group of permanent deacons are presented for ordination in the 1970's.

and clergy, worked through political channels to effect major civil rights legislation. In so doing, Catholics were responding to the judgment made in the U.S. bishops' 1958 statement that "segregation in our country has led to oppressive conditions and the denial of basic human rights...in the fundamental fields of education, job opportunity and housing." Such Catholic senators as Eugene McCarthy and Robert Kennedy (assassinated in 1968) became particularly visible leaders in the fight for racial justice.

On the raging issue of the Vietnam War, the moral issues did not appear clear-cut to most Americans. Many Catholics in particular, accustomed for generations to loyal patriotic support of the country's wars, found the decision to challenge national purposes wrenching. Again, large numbers of Catholics took to the streets and the political process to protest the war. Some, such as Fathers Philip and Daniel Berrigan and the "Catonsville Nine" undertook more dramatic forms of opposition, breaking into a draft board and burning files with homemade napalm. Other Catholics followed the lead of Cardinal Spellman of New York, head of the Military Ordinariate (now the Archdiocese for Military Services), in their persistent support of the administration's war aims.

In 1968, the Catholic bishops of the United States had spoken in measured terms of the Vietnam involvement, admitting the rights of those who dissented and urging the option of selective conscientious objection even as they found warrant for the conflict in the just war argument. In 1971 the bishops released another, more far-reaching statement in which they maintained that "whatever good we hope to achieve through continued involvement in this war is now outweighed by the destruction of human life and of the moral values which it entails" (*Resolution on Southeast Asia*).

In a quiet way, this was a revolutionary moment in the long annals of official Catholic support of national policy. "For the first time in modern history," historian David O'Brien writes in *Public Catholicism*, "a body of national bishops, during a war, had publicly judged their government's actions unjust." This prophetic challenge to national mores was but a foreshadowing of others to come: from the strong Catholic resistance to the 1973 *Roe v. Wade* Supreme Court decision permitting abortion down to the cautionary letter the American bishops wrote to President George Bush on the very eve of the 1991 war in the Persian Gulf.

The papal encyclical *Humanae Vitae* of 1968, which maintained the traditional ban on artificial contraception, was endorsed by the American Catholic bishops in a pastoral letter that stressed the need for patience and understanding. But many American Catholics, schooled in newer traditions of challenging national and ecclesiastical policies, resisted the teaching.

Several clerical theologians across the country signed

Profiling U.S. Catholics

Five words describing ways in which Catholic religious worldviews vary somewhat from those of some other religious groups:

1) Intellectual: more likely to try to reconcile faith and reason.
2) Accepting: more understanding attitude toward sinners.
3) Pragmatic: marked by intense concern with this world.
4) Communal: greater emphasis on social justice as a dimension of faith.
5) Private: not intensely concerned about converting others. Evangelization became an articulated theme in American Catholicism only in the 1980's and 1990's.

Five perceptions about modern American Catholics that are demonstrably false:

1) Religious activity is declining dramatically.
2) Young Catholics are permanently leaving the Church in a mass exodus.
3) The more educated Catholics become, the more likely they are to leave the Church.
4) Catholic women are in a state of revolt against the Church.
5) Catholics have grown more conservative as they have grown more affluent.

Five areas in which Catholics have been on the cutting edge of social change in American society:

1) Tolerance
2) Women's rights
3) Communal dimension of society
4) Balancing power in presidential politics
5) Peace issues

From *The American Catholic People*, by George Gallup, Jr., and Jim Castelli

Cesar Chavez organized the United Farm Workers of America and orchestrated a nationwide boycott of California table grapes.

statements of carefully worded dissent. In Washington, D.C., some fifty priests took a position of public opposition and many were suspended by Cardinal Patrick O'Boyle; such action was the exception rather than the rule. Meanwhile, a sizable majority of America's married Catholics, according to consistent polls taken across two decades, declined to incorporate the papal teaching into their personal lives. The crisis of conscience caused some to turn away from the Church and gave rise among others to a selective approach to the Church's teaching sometimes called "cafeteria Catholicism."

Controversy within and without the Church did not deter American Catholics from expending moral and religious energies on many fronts. The Campaign for Human Development was established in 1969 to combat injustice and poverty through the funding of self-help programs carried out by poor and affluent alike. The Catholic Committee on Urban Ministry (CCUM) was formed in 1967 and Network in 1971, both to further social justice. Call to Action sessions in dioceses across America in the 1970's attempted to identify issues and priorities for both Church and nation through a broad consultation process.

Labor expert and columnist Monsignor George Higgins and farm worker Cesar Chavez (1927-1993) continued the Catholic tradition of championing the cause of workers. Many American Catholics in these years protested their government's involvement with the *contras* of Nicaragua. The 1981 killing of four American Catholic women working in the missions of El Salvador, coming just a year after the murder of Salvadoran Archbishop Oscar Romero, shocked the nation.

Catholics were especially prominent in the prolife movement. By the late 1980's, especially after the 1989 Supreme Court decision *Webster v. Reproductive Health Services* returned some discretion to the states in abortion issues, a further debate raged over the growing number of Catholic political leaders who distinguished between personal opposition to abortion and public policy.

Meanwhile, the bishops of the United States took public stands on scores of issues, advocating more federally-supported low-income housing and handgun control, aid to developing nations, and opposing abortion and capital punishment. This wide range of concern was designated by Cardinal Joseph Bernardin as a "consistent life ethic" of Catholic concern for

Abortion protesters demonstrate in their concern for the life of the unborn.

For Discussion

Discuss Cardinal Bernardin's "consistent life ethic." How does it affect your political activity?

the enhancement of life at all levels. In keeping with this tradition, the American Catholic bishops issued two controversial pastoral letters in the 1980's: *The Challenge of Peace* (1983), questioning the morality of nuclear weapons, and *Economic Justice for All* (1986), stressing a "preferential option for the poor" in economic and political matters.

In the area of interfaith relations, postconciliar Catholics joined readily with Protestant and Jewish neighbors in worship and social services. People of various faiths met informally in living rooms, formed formal covenants between their congregations and established comprehensive neighborhood ministries to serve the social needs of their area. At the theological level, official dialogues were undertaken between Catholic theologians and those of other traditions: Episcopalian, Lutheran, Methodist, Orthodox, Presbyterian, Southern Baptist and the Disciples of Christ. Over twenty official joint declarations have come forth from such gatherings, honestly expressing both commonality and differences.

Such Catholic thinkers as Raymond Brown, S.S., Avery Dulles, S.J., and David Tracy continued to probe the depths of Catholic tradition as it came face-to-face with modern experience in a pluralistic context. One of the more controversial figures in Catholic theological circles was a moralist, Father Charles Curran of the Catholic University. Without challenge to his priestly standing, Curran was ordered removed by Rome from the Washington faculty in 1986 because he questioned traditional teaching in sexual areas (birth control, homosexuality and the indissolubility of marriage).

The presence of so many theologians perceived as liberal has been challenged throughout the postconciliar period by such groups as the Catholics United for the Faith (founded in 1968) and the Fellowship of Catholic Scholars (1978). According to historian James Hennesey, many Catholics after the Council were pained by a loss of stability, and "appalled at gaucheries which passed for liturgical reform. Many missed the musical and artistic splendor, the sense of solemnity and awe." Many commentators in both Catholic and secular press maintained that a "Catholic Restoration" began after the election of Pope John Paul II in 1978, seeking to stem (especially through episcopal appointment) excessive or overly rapid change.

In the realm of spirituality, Catholics in record numbers turned to adult religious education, especially the study of Scripture. The Cursillo and Marriage Encounter movements both flourished. After 1967, a Catholic charismatic movement arose as well, with major centers at Duquesne and Notre Dame universities. By the mid-1980's, an estimated half-million Catholics were involved. Parishes turned to such programs as RENEW as updated versions of the parish mission.

Traditional piety to the Blessed Virgin Mary (highlighted by the formal opening of the National Shrine of the Immaculate Conception in Washington in 1959) continued strong in

American Catholicism, though not as predominantly as before the Council. In particular, ethnic celebrations of Mary (Our Lady of Czestochowa among Poles, Our Lady of Guadalupe among Hispanics) remained as deep expressions of traditional piety. By the late 1980's, thousands of American Catholics were jetting to Yugoslavia to venerate the reputed Marian apparitions at Medjugorje.

As part of a general movement that gained considerable ground in America from the 1960's onward, a range of Catholic feminist voices arose in the postconciliar era. Among the best-known were Rosemary Radford Ruether and Elisabeth Schüssler Fiorenza. At issue were a considerable array of concerns (besides the question considered a closed topic by Pope John Paul II—the ordination of women): women's rights and roles in decisionmaking in Church and society, the use of inclusive language in the liturgy, the shaping of spirituality and images of God. New organizations of American Catholic women came into existence, including the Women's Ordination Conference in 1976 and the WomenChurch movement in 1983.

Besides the questions raised by feminists, Catholics in America found any number of issues matters of sharp debate: greater involvement in the selection of bishops, the resources expended on Catholic schools, the treatment of homosexuals and divorced people in the Catholic community, the grounds for and accessibility of marriage annulments, the law of celibacy, the declining numbers of priests and religious, ministerial "burnout," uniform catechetical instruction, pedophiliac priests.

The list could go on at length. A widely quoted *USA Today*, CNN/Gallup poll conducted at the time of Pope John Paul II's visit to World Youth Day in Denver, Colorado, in August 1993 produced some startling figures. While seventy-three percent of American Catholics approved of the pope's handling of his office, seventy-nine percent also said that they followed their own consciences rather than papal pronouncements on difficult moral issues. Additionally, eighty-four percent disagreed with the Vatican teaching on birth control; seventy-six percent favored allowing married priests; sixty-three percent supported the ordination of women. The very mention of many of these topics would have shocked earlier generations of American Catholics out of their wits.

In his remarks to the bishops of the United States, Pope

Feminist theologian Elisabeth Schüssler Fiorenza questions the status accorded women within the Church.

Pope John Paul II welcomes one of the twenty thousand young people who attended World Youth Day in Denver in 1993.

John Paul II called the Church in America "vital and dynamic." Yet he deplored the "false morality" of the modern world, and referred to abortion and euthanasia as the "slaughter of the innocents." "Many Catholics," he insisted, "are in danger of losing their faith." In what may have been the most solemn observation made on his trip, the pope added that "America

An Appalachian Song

Dear sisters and brothers,
we urge all of you...
to be a part of the rebirth of utopias,
to recover and defend the struggling dream....
For it is the weak things of this world,
which seem like folly,
that the Spirit takes up
and makes its own.
The dream of the mountains' struggle,
the dream of simplicity
and of justice,
like so many other repressed visions,
is, we believe, the voice of the Lord among us.

In taking them up,
hopefully the Church
might once again be known as

—a center of the Spirit,
—a place where poetry dares to speak,
—where the song reigns unchallenged
—where art flourishes,
—where nature is welcome,
—where little people and little needs come first,
—where justice speaks loudly,
—where in a wilderness of idolatrous destruction
  the great voice of God still cries out for life.

(From *This Land Is Home to Me*, Pastoral Letter of
Catholic Bishops in Appalachia, 1975)

needs much prayer lest it lose its soul."

The Catholics who today constitute about twenty-five percent of the American population are a people who have moved decidedly up the economic and social ladder. On April 8, 1990, *The New York Times* religion editor Peter Steinfels reported that "Catholic descendants of earlier immigrants are now ensconced in the middle and higher ranks of government, business and the professions." Catholic authors are well known in American letters: from the novels of sociologist Father Andrew Greeley to those of Mary Gordon, William Kennedy and the late Walker Percy.

The complexion of Catholic Americans has changed dramatically in the last generation as well. By 1990, it was estimated that nearly eighty percent of the twenty-two million Hispanics in America were baptized Roman Catholic. Even though this group seems especially vulnerable to the attraction of fundamentalist sects, Hispanic Catholics currently constitute at least twenty percent of all American Catholics. There are now twenty-one American bishops of Hispanic origin; in at least a dozen dioceses, Hispanics make up more than half the Catholic population.

The number of African-American Catholics in America has also risen: about a million and a half, with twelve black bishops on the national scene. A national Black Catholic Clergy Caucus was formed in 1968, and a national Office for Black Catholics in 1970. In the wake of the war in Southeast Asia, large numbers of Vietnamese Catholics immigrated to the United States.

In three trips to the mainland United States (1979, 1987 and 1993), Pope John Paul II has seen for himself the wide diversity in American Catholicism. The pontiff has journeyed from Boston to Alaska, from Iowa to Arizona. At the time of the 1987 visit, Joseph Berger, writing for *The New York Times*, found a new, encouraging mood in both pontiff and people. In short compass, Berger's remarks suggest the transformed texture of American Catholicism in the generation after the Second Vatican Council:

> *The collective image was of a plucky people who need to speak their mind because they feel so passionate about the church itself and want to see it as fine as it can be. It was, says [Eugene] Kennedy, the courage of adult*

For Discussion

What would you say are the most serious challenges facing the Church today? The greatest possibilities?

children talking to a parent they love, but also know
they must confront if they are going to maintain their
own integrity. The fact that the parent let them talk and
listened left behind a sense of vibrancy that may gratify
the church's establishment and dissenters alike.

Conclusion

The Catholic Gift

To look at American Catholicism over nearly five hundred years is also to glimpse the nature of religion at large in this sprawling land. Three recent books in particular have provided excellent insights into the ongoing religious instinct in American life.

The first of these, *The People's Religion*, by George Gallup, Jr. and Jim Castelli (1989), reports that for all their materialism, secularity and misplaced intensities, Americans remain a remarkably religiously oriented people. In national surveys, well above ninety percent describe themselves as believers in God; over half of the population goes into a house of worship in a typical month. American believers, report the authors, are more pragmatic, pluralistic and therapeutic in approaching religion than their ancestors were. They also tend to separate belief and belonging: They often do not feel a need for a specific denomination. But overall, Americans remain a people for whom religious—even mystical—experience forms a persistent value.

Veteran Catholic sociologist Andrew Greeley has made a searching study of his coreligionists in a 1990 study entitled *The Catholic Myth*, a lively text full of intriguing detail and occasional surprises. The distinctive trait of Catholics, the largest religious group in America, Greeley maintains, is their sacramental imagination—their ability to "imagine God as present in the world and the world as revelatory instead of bleak." Ritual and reverence, ceremony and celebration capture and enliven the Catholic heart.

If Gallup, Castelli and Greeley all find a strong yearning and respect for religious experience in modern America, that fact comes as no surprise to Robert Bellah and four other professionals who collaborated on the landmark 1985 study of American values, *Habits of the Heart*. After intensive analysis and extensive interviews, the writers concluded that Americans have not found "a life devoted to personal ambition and consumerism satisfactory, and most are seeking in one way or another to transcend the limitations of a self-centered life." As a people, they hunger for communities of memory and hope in which they can find coherence and continuity.

It would surely not be wide of the mark to suggest that these very hungers have been a driving force in the life of American Catholics, no matter how they may at times have faltered. Formed by an ancient tradition that seeks to balance faith and reason, nature and grace, discipline and freedom, tradition and creativity, they have sought to create comprehensive communities of hope and memory on the American landscape. When such communities are at their best, they ennoble and nurture, foster compassion and justice, and situate the individual in the context of the mystery of God.

As we began this survey, we noted the tendency of some late nineteenth-century Catholics to find such possibilities in their faith alone, and to urge an energetic push for mass conversions. We now know much better that neither Catholics nor any other group have a monopoly of all powers for good. But they do have an inestimable heritage of mind and heart, faith and community, toleration and self-scrutiny to contribute to the pluralism of American faith and life.

Catholics are a people who know the power of roots and reach, of ritual and forgiveness. They carry about as their heritage timeless stories of courage, self-sacrifice and endurance. They also bear the scars of their own collective sins, their failures to incorporate and manifest their own goals and ideals. If these same Catholics can allow the "sleeping giant" in them to come to birth by listening and learning, teaching and serving, being both humble and assured, they will never cease to be a benediction to the United States.

They will help their nation, itself both great and flawed, to walk a road true to its own best instincts and traditions. Well-walked, that road can make liberty and justice for all less of a slogan and more of a reality. That difficult and winding road can lead a people in directions they need to go: from chaos to cosmos, from coldness to compassion, from despair to destiny.

Bibliography

Ahlstrom, Sydney. *A Religious History of the American People*. (New Haven: Yale University Press, 1972).

Albanese, Catherine. *America: Religions and Religion*. (Belmont, Ca.: Wadsworth Publishing Co., 1992).

Beck, Melinda. "The Lost Worlds of Ancient America," *Newsweek* Special Edition, "When Worlds Collide," Fall 1991.)

Bellah, Robert, et. al. *Habits of the Heart*. (New York: HarperCollins, 1985).

Carey, Patrick. *American Catholic Religious Thought*. (New York: Paulist Press, 1987).

Chinnici, Joseph. *Living Stones: The History and Structure of Catholic Spiritual Life in the United States*. (New York: Macmillan Publishing Co., 1989).

Davis, Cyprian. *The History of Black Catholics in the United States*. (New York: Crossroad, 1990).

Dolan, Jay. *The American Catholic Experience*. (Garden City, N.Y.: Image Books, 1985).

_____. *Catholic Revivalism*. (Notre Dame, Ind.: University of Notre Dame Press, 1978).

Ellis, John Tracy. *American Catholicism*. (Chicago: University of Chicago Press, 1969).

_____ (ed.) *Documents of American Catholic History*. 3 vols. (Wilmington, Del.: Michael Glazier, 1987).

Fogarty, Gerald (ed.). *Patterns of Episcopal Leadership*. (New York: Macmillan Publishing Co., 1989).

_____ (ed.). *The Vatican and the American Hierarchy From 1870 to 1965*. (Wilmington, Del.: Michael Glazier, 1985).

Gallup, George and Castelli, Jim. *The People's Religion*. (New York: Macmillan Publishing Co., 1989).

Glazier, Michael (ed.), *Where We Are: American Catholics in the 1980's*. (Wilmington, Del.: Michael Glazier, 1985).

Gleason, Philip. *Keeping the Faith: American Catholicism Past and Present*. (Notre Dame, Ind.: University of Notre Dame Press, 1987).

Greeley, Andrew. *The Catholic Myth*. (New York: Charles Scribners' Sons, 1990).

Halsey, William. *The Survival of American Innocence*. (Notre Dame, Ind.: University of Notre Dame Press, 1980).

Handy, Robert. *A History of the Churches in the United States and Canada*. (New York: Oxford University Press, 1977).

Hennesey, James. *American Catholics*. (New York: Oxford University Press, 1981).

Kenneally, James. *The History of American Catholic Women*. (New York: Crossroad, 1990).

Kennelly, Karen (ed.). *American Catholic Women: A Historical Exploration*. (New York: Macmillan Publishing Co., 1989).

Liptak, Dolores. *Immigrants and Their Church*. (New York: Macmillan Publishing Co., 1989).

Marsden, George. *Fundamentalism and American Culture*. (New York: Oxford University Press, 1980).

Marty, Martin. *Pilgrims in their Own Land: 500 Years of Religion in America*. (Boston: Little, Brown & Co., Inc., 1984).

McNickle, D'Arcy. "American Indians" in the 1987 *Collier's Encyclopedia* (Vol. 12).

Noll, Mark. *A History of Christianity in the United States and Canada*. (Grand Rapids: Wm. B. Eerdmans Publishing Co., 1992).

O'Brien, David. *Public Catholicism*. (New York: Macmillan Publishing Co., 1989).

Reher, Margaret Mary. *Catholic Intellectual Life in America*. (New York: Macmillan Publishing Co., 1989).

Spalding, Thomas. *The Premier See*. (Baltimore: The Johns Hopkins University Press, 1989).

Taves, Ann. *The Household of Faith*. (Notre Dame, Ind.: University of Notre Dame Press, 1986).

White, Joseph. *The Diocesan Seminary in the United States*. (Notre Dame, Ind.: University of Notre Dame Press, 1989).

Index

abolitionism 54
abortion 147, 149, 153
Accademia 97
activism 98, 128
Adams, John 52
Adams, Sam 48
Alabama 30
alcoholism 81
Allouez, Claude, S.J. 29
America 117, 137
"America the Beautiful" 111
American Catholic Historical
   Association 110
*American Ecclesiastical
   Review* 109
American Federation of Labor
   (AFL) 110, 128
American Protective
   Association 122
Americanism 101
Americanists 97
Amish 40
Anglicans 35, 47
Anti-Catholicism 39, 44-45,
   48, 64, 74, 122, 132, 135
anti-immigrant violence 77
anti-Semitism 132
apostolic delegate 100
Appalachia 7
architecture 78
Arizona 17, 20, 50
Ark 40
armed forces 120, 134
Association of Catholic Trade
   Unionists (ACTU) 127
atomic bomb 134
Ave Maria 109

Back of the Yards
   Neighborhood Council 130
Badin, Stephen 55, 67
Baltimore Catechism 103
Baltimore 23, 50, 59, 124

Baltimore, Lord 40, 44
Baltimore, plenary councils
   of 63
Baltimore, provincial councils
   of 63
Baltimore, Second Plenary
   Council of 90, 93
Baltimore, Third Plenary
   Council of 102
Banning, Margaret Culkin 118
Baptists 39, 47, 65
Baraga, Frederic 70
Bardstown, diocese of 59, 65
Barry, John 49
Bates, Katherine Lee 111
Beecher, Henry Ward 110
Bell, Lawrence H. 101
Bellah, Robert 157
Benedict, St. 81
Benedictine 81, 128
Berle, Milton 135
Bernardin, Joseph 149
Berrigan, Daniel 147
Berrigan, Philip 147
Biblical studies 94, 141
Bill of Rights 55
Biloxi 30
Birth control 118, 145, 147,
   151
Bishops' Program of Social
   Reconstruction 120
Black Catholic Clergy
   Caucus 155
black Catholics 92, 109, 132,
   155
blacks, freed 90
Blanshard, Paul 135
Borden, Lucille Papin 118
Boston 49, 53, 75, 124
Boston, diocese of 59
Bozzell, L. Brent 136
Brent, Margaret 43
"brick and mortar" era 107, 115

Jones, Mary Harris
  ("Mother") 110, 119
justice 128

Kant 48
Kaskaskia 30-31
Keane, John J. 97, 100
Kelly, Honest John 109
Kennedy, Eugene 155
Kennedy, John Fitzgerald 139,
  142
Kennedy, Robert 146
Kennedy, William 155
Kenrick, Francis Patrick 68,
  85, 87
Kentucky 31, 64
Kerby, William 119
Kilmer, Joyce 119
King, Martin Luther, Jr. 145
Kino, Eusebio Francisco 20, 28
Kirk, Russell 136
Knights of Columbus 109
Knights of Labor 102
Knights of Peter Claver 109
Knights of St. John 109
Ku Klux Klan 122-123

labor 98, 102, 119, 122, 127-
  128, 149
Labor unions 102, 110
LaFarge, John 132
Laity 62, 98, 127-130, 142,
  145
Leavenworth 103
Lee, Mary Digges 50
letters 150
Liberal 101, 151
liberalism 98
Lincoln 86
Lippmann, Walter 125
Lithuanians 105
liturgical 144
liturgical reform 151
liturgical renewal 128, 139
liturgy 130, 141-142, 152
Locke, John 48
Los Angeles 23
Louisiana 30, 68
Louisiana Purchase 63, 68
Louisville 77, 83

Lowell, Robert 139
Loyola 82
Luce, Clare Booth 135
Lukas, John 136
Lutheran 47
Lynch, Patrick 87

Maine 25
manifest destiny 38, 70, 98
Manso, Alonso 15
Margil, Antonio 20
Maritain, Raissa 128
Maritain, Jacques 128
Marquette, Jacques, S.J. 26,
  28, 29, 118
Marriage Encounter 151
Marx, Karl 94
Mary 151
Maryknoll 117
Maryland 42, 49
Maréchal, Ambrose 64
Massachusetts Bay Colony 36
Maurin, Peter 128, 130
Mayflower 35
Mazzuchelli, Samuel 70
McCalla, Sara 49
McCarthy, Eugene 146
McCarthy, Joseph 137
McCloskey, John 124
McGill, John 87
McGlynn, Edward 97
McGowan, Raymond 127
McMaster, James 86
McNicholas, John T. 127
McQuaid, Bernard 98
Medjugorje 152
Menard, René, S.J. 29
Menendez, Pedro 17
Merton, Thomas 68, 82, 135,
  139
*Messenger of the Sacred
  Heart* 109
Methodist 39, 85
Meurin, Sebastian, S.J. 30
Mexican War 70
Mexicans 105
Meyer, Albert 141
Michel, Virgil 128
Michigan 28, 31, 70
Mill Hill Fathers 91

Milwaukee 73, 105
Minnesota 25
mission, parish 107, 151
missionaries 70
Missionary Oblates of Mary 12
missions 10, 13, 16-17, 20, 21,
  30-31, 117
Mississippi 30
Missouri 30
Mobile 30
Modernism 101
modernity 93-94
Mohawks 26-27
Monasticism 81
Monk, Maria 75
Monte Casino 134
Mooney, Edward 132
Morse, Samuel F.B. 75
Moylan, Stephen 49
Mundelein, George 124
Murphy, Frank 133
Murray, John Courtney 44,
  136, 141
Murray, Philip 128

Nashville 68
National Catholic Conference
  for Interracial Justice 132
*National Catholic
  Reporter* 144
National Catholic Rural Life
  Conference 119
National Catholic War
  Council 120
National Catholic Welfare
  Conference 120, 127
National Catholic Women's
  Union 109
National Conference of
  Catholic Charities 119
National Conference of
  Catholic Men 119
National Conference of
  Catholic Women 119
National parishes 107
National Shrine of the
  Immaculate Conception 151
Native Americans 7-14, 23, 40,
  70
Nazism 133

Sisters of Charity of
  Nazareth 68
Sisters of Loretto 67
Sisters of St. Joseph of
  Carondolet 91
Slavery 43, 47, 81, 83, 85
Slovaks 105
Smet, Pierre de 70
Smith, Alfred Emanuel 122
social action 122, 127
social gospel 110, 119
social justice 95, 142, 149
Society of the Sacred Heart 68
Spalding, Catherine 68
Spalding, Martin John 68, 76-
  77, 89, 97-98, 101
Spanish 10, 15-25, 30, 35, 41,
  50, 53
Spanish Civil War 132
Spanish-American War 101
Spellman, Francis 136, 141,
  147
St. Anthony Messenger 109
St. Augustine 17, 23
St. Francis de Sales 25
St. Ignatius Loyola 15
St. Jane Frances de Chantal 25
St. John of the Cross 15
St. Louis 30-31, 68-69, 73, 141
St. Louis parish 30
St. Louis University 69
St. Mary of the Lake 124
St. Meinrad 82
St. Teresa of Avila 15
St. Vincent de Paul 25
St. Vincent de Paul
  Society 109
Statuary Hall 28
Stowe, Harriet Beecher 89
Sulpicians 25, 31, 52, 67
Supreme Court 83, 122, 132-
  133, 135, 147, 149
Sylvester, Henry 137

Tablet 137
Tammany Hall 109
Taney, Roger Brooke 83, 85
Tarry, Ellen 132
Tegananokoa, Stephen 27
Tekakwitha, Kateri 28

Texas 17, 20
Thayer, John 54
Tobin, Mary Luke 141
toleration 7, 37, 40, 42
Toleration, Maryland Act of 41-
  42
Toussaint, Pierre 59
Tracy, David 151
Transcendentalism 77
Trappists 68, 81, 139
Treaty of Paris 30
Trinity College 83
Truman 135
trusteeism 54, 61, 64, 67-68
Turner, Thomas Wyatt 132

U.S. Catholic Historical
  Society 110
Ukrainians 105
unions 127-128
Unitarian 80
United Nations 143
University of Michigan 70
University of Notre Dame 77
University of San Francisco 82
Ursulines 30, 52

Valesh, Eva MacDonald 110
Vietnam 139, 145, 147
Vietnamese 155
Vincennes 30, 68
Vincentians 68
Voltaire 48

Wanderer, The 144
Washington 97, 123, 149, 151
Washington, George 49, 52
Wateus, Mary 50
Whelan, James 87
White, Andrew 40
Whitfield, George 47
Whitfield, James 64
Whitman, Walt 77
William and Mary 44
Williams, Michael 117, 128
Williams, Roger 37, 44
Willis, Gary 136
Wimmer, Boniface 81
Winthrop, John 36, 38
Wisconsin 29

witchcraft 38
Wolff, Mary Madeleva 139
Women 60, 81, 83, 110, 119-
  120, 152
Women's suffrage 119-120
Women, ordination of 152
WomenChurch 152
World Parliament of
  Religions 99
World War I 119, 124
World War II 132, 134, 137

Xavierian Brothers 104

Yorke, Peter 119
Young Catholic Students 129
Young Christian Workers 129

Sources of Illustrations

Abbey of Gethsemani Archives, 80; Air Force Museum, 126;
Archdiocese of Baltimore Archives, 108; Archdiocese of Chicago
Archives and Records Center, 129, 133; Archives of the Sisters of
Charity of Cincinnati, Ohio, 19, 61, 69, 89; Archives, Sisters of
Loretto, 91; The Archives of the University of Notre Dame, 26, 46, 54,
55, 58, 63, 68, 75, 78, 79, 82, 84, 87, 92, 98, 101, 103, 104, 109, 114,
118, 121, 123, 124, 134, 136, 152; Bureau of Catholic Indian
Missions, 13; Catholic News Service 11, 140, 143, 146, 149, 150, 153;
Center for Migration Studies, 96; Lyons Collection/Bellarmine
College, 67; Marquette University Archives/Memorial Library, 131;
Maryknoll Missioners, 117; North Wind Picture Archives, 24, 29, 34,
36, 44, 56, 72; Philadelphia Archdiocesan Historical Research Center,
42; Sulpician Archives, Baltimore, 53, 60; photo by Catherine Walsh,
6; photos by Jack Wintz, O.F.M., 14, 17.